To Ian,
with
love

Jaya a
John

1986

# —COMPLETE—
# JAPANESE
# —COOKBOOK—

# COMPLETE JAPANESE COOKBOOK

YOKO KOBAYASHI

HAMLYN

**For Stuart, Nancy, Jean and especially my husband, Bill**

### Other titles in this series:

*Complete Indian Cookbook*
*Florence Greenberg's Jewish Cookbook*
*The Mexican Cookbook*
*Cooking with a Wok*
*Regional Chinese Cookbook*

Photography by Martin Brigdale
Illustrations by Bobbie Colgate-Stone

Published 1985 by
Hamlyn Publishing
Bridge House, London Road
Twickenham, Middlesex, England

© Hamlyn Publishing 1985
a division of The Hamlyn Publishing Group Ltd

ISBN 0 600 32470 2

Photoset in Apollo Roman
by Tameside Filmsetting Limited, Lancashire

Printed in Spain

# Contents

# History and Philosophy of Japanese Food

In order to fully appreciate the taste and texture of Japanese food it is important to know a little about the history and thinking behind the diverse styles and flavours which are characteristic of Japanese cuisine. For example, if you prepare an exotic dinner party from this book it will be useful to be able to answer your guests' questions about the origins of the recipes and the manner in which they are served.

Japanese life is still more formal than western culture and this is especially true in the case of food and eating habits. There is great significance attached to the serving of any one particular dish and the way in which the food is arranged is equally important. A western cook is unlikely to be able to copy this in a truly authentic fashion but this introduction provides a basic historical framework for understanding these culinary traditions.

### The Prehistoric Age
### (approximately 8000 BC–AD 57)

There is no firmly established theory about the origin of the Japanese nation; however, some facts are known from the remains left by early inhabitants of the islands. The current oriental inhabitants of Japan were not the original natives. The recognisably Japanese people arrived in Japan from Korea and, probably, from islands in the Pacific. The native Caucasian inhabitants (*Ainu*) had a rather primitive culture: they lived in caves in winter and made nests in the trees in summer. They were predominantly hunters and fishermen and they wore furs. Earthen vessels (*Jyomon shiki* and *yayoi shiki doki*) and wooden pots were made to serve as containers. These people also discovered fire by rubbing pieces of wood together, so they ate boiled food as well as raw food.

Cereals, fish, seaweeds, vegetables and meat were eaten, and rice was prepared in a *kowameshi* style – unpolished rice steamed in

a basket (*ii*) or boiled in water (*kayu*). It is clear that their diet consisted of marine mammals, fish, birds (chicken, snipe, wild goose, sparrow or wild duck) and animal meat (rabbit, wild bear or deer). They also made use of bamboo shoots, chives and ginger at this time. People used tweezer-shaped chopsticks made from bamboo and tied together at the top with straw.

### AD 300–700

Japan and Korea communicated with each other since ancient times but this increased and the transfer of culture became very intense from about 700 AD, bringing with it a high standard of living to Japan. Korea was considerably influenced by China, and Korean culture reached a high peak at this time. The Korean innovator *Niho* introduced *sake* – making to Japan; prior to this the Japanese brewed a very crude form of alcohol using techniques which would not make good reading in a cookery book.

Two very important Chinese influences reached Japan at this time: Buddhism and Confucianism. These religions (or philosophies) had a dramatic effect on food in Japan. Buddhism prohibited the killing of animals, so monks and nuns of this religion followed a vegetarian (or at least meatless) diet known as *kosei shojin*.

### AD 700–1000

During this period direct communication started between Japan and China. Many Chinese recipes and cooking techniques were imported, then used alongside the older Japanese methods. Gradually, the Chinese techniques were subtly changed until they became identifiably Japanese.

### Early *Asuka, Nara* Age (AD 593–784)

People started to use *hishio* (original soy sauce) at this time; but not as a dipping sauce for fish and meat– this use of soy sauce is a

6

relatively modern idea. The oldest established and uniquely Japanese cookery style is *namasu tsukuru* using fresh raw fish. The style is the basis of the current cookery technique *namasu*, in which raw or grilled ingredients are mixed with rice wine. The *sashimi* style of food preparation is also derived from *namasu tsukuru*.

In the middle of the ninth century a settled pattern of Japanese cookery and food etiquette emerged, drawing mainly on Chinese ideals. Some specific techniques which evolved are *hocho shiki* – a technique using a knife, later to become *shijo ryu* – and *kyo o zen* – arranging a table for a dinner party, New Year's Day and other seasonal festivals. These techniques are documented in certain early books.

The Japanese were eating polished rice, wheat and millet at this time. They made *mochi* from glutinous rice (as they still do now) and shaped it into round cakes to offer to the gods. People believed that the circle shape was perfect and sacred so they refused to cut up the *mochi* after using it as an offering; instead they left the *mochi* until it became hard, then broke it up with a hammer. The pieces were grilled, and called *kake mochi* – they were the original rice crackers. There is no truth in the story that the name *mochi* arose because it requires so MUCH chewing!

## AD 900–1300

People started to make *sushi* during this age. The word *sushi* means having a sour, acidic flavour. The idea for *sushi* originated from the habits of the *misago* seabirds: they caught fish and hid them behind rocks. These were kept damp by the waves and they turned naturally sour. The fishermen used to collect the fish and people ate them: this was natural *sushi*. A little later, cooks began to make artificial *sushi* (*ichiya zushi*) by cutting open the sour fish and stuffing them with cooked rice. The acid flavour spread through the rice which was then eaten.

## The Introduction of Tea (AD 1185–1573)

Zen monks spent long periods of time in meditation and they found that it was difficult to stay fully awake, so tea was used as a means of promoting wakefulness. It was believed that tea had many beneficial properties – extending life, improving health or acting as a tranquilliser, for example. Japanese green tea is rich in both vitamins B and C, so some of these old ideas may have some basis in fact.

Tea became central to many forms of entertainment and was indispensable for social gatherings. When tea was drunk with a light snack it became known as *kaiseki*. It had a far more important ritualistic role in Zen life and this role eventually led to the famous tea ceremony known as *chakai*.

## Kamakura **Age (AD 1192–1333)**

During this age the warrior culture of Japan – *Samurai* – emerged. Cooking became simpler and there was considerable development of ideas for food which was suitable for taking into battle conditions. In contrast, it became normal for Japanese people to eat three meals each day whereas previously only two meals were eaten.

The *shojin ryori* cookery style developed during this era to complement Buddhist beliefs. This cookery style uses ingredients like vegetables, seaweed and processed dried foods. Fish and meat were considered to be smelly ingredients by the followers of this school and they avoided them.

The *shojin ryori* cookery style spread very widely to the common people as Buddhism grew more popular during the *Kamakura* age. However, vegetarianism was not observed very strictly by the common people (or by the warrior class) and some meat as well as a form of cheese were widely eaten.

## Muromachi **Age (AD 1334–1573)**

It was during this era that the feudal system rose to a peak. Cooking techniques became more artistic, mirroring in many ways the growing sophistication of the *Samurai* class, and there were many rules which governed how each food tray should be arranged.

These styles of food preparation were very complex and they are now very rare but the basic ideas still survive in *kaiseki* – the tea party meal – and *kaiseki ryori* – the meal for drinking *sake*.

### *Azuchi Momoyama* **Age (AD 1575–1600)**

Japanese culture was predominantly influenced by the *Samurai* class during this age. Simplicity and asceticism were regarded as prime virtues.

The word *kaiseki* comes from Zen. In order to endure going without food in winter, monks and soldiers used to heat a stone, then put it inside their clothes. The word used for this is *kaiseki*: in Zen language this word means supper.

During this era contact was made with Europeans, especially traders and missionaries. Their influence on Japan was profound, particularly in culinary aspects. Most of the initial contact was with Portuguese and Spanish sailors and the Japanese term for their exotic food was *namban ryori*. *Tempura* is probably the most important example of this importation of technique and it is based directly on Portuguese cooking methods of that time. *Tempura* means frying vegetables and fish very rapidly in oil, using a thin coating of batter to protect the food. Traditionally, the Japanese already fried food but without batter; so this innovation produced a whole range of new dishes. These are well represented in this book because they are especially suitable for the western palate.

As well as new cooking techniques the Europeans introduced a whole range of new ingredients from China and Europe itself; for example corn, chillies, pumpkin, watermelon, *ganmodoki* (bean curd with vegetables), potatoes, sugar, pepper and *sansyo* (Japanese pepper), castella (sponge cake), confeitos (solid sugar), alfeloa (like sugar), marmelo (plant seeds), biscuits and bread. Interest in sweet dishes increased at this time and this is reflected in the short chapter included in this book. Japanese sweets were made from *azuki* (red beans), sugar, glutinous rice and plain flour as well as other ingredients. They were very similar to today's sweets and there were also speciality sweets available in most of the prefectures in Japan, just as there are now. For example, *Mie* prefecture is famous for *seki no to* and *naga mochi*; *Aichi* prefecture has *tsukubane fuji dango*, *tokyo-kaminari okoshi*, *osaka-awa okoshi* and *yokan*.

### The *Edo* **Age (AD 1603–1867)**

The Japanese rulers closed the country to all foreigners for about 200 years during this age, but Japanese cookery still accomplished a great deal in this isolated period. One reason for this was the emergence of many licensed restaurants, often centred around various forms of entertainment.

Tea shops began to appear and many were built in the red-light district or entertainment areas of major cities and towns. The licensed restaurants provided an alternative which were more suitable for entertaining guests so many tea shops were eventually converted to this role. The present style of *sushi* was developed at about this time, exemplified by pressed *sushi* (*oshi zushi*) and small rice ball *sushi* (*nigiri zushi*).

### *Meiji* **Era (AD 1868–1911)**

In this era Japan underwent an unprecedented revolution, which turned it from a purely feudal, powerless state into an industrial giant virtually within a generation. The country was opened to foreigners and the Japanese government enthusiastically encouraged the importation of all that they felt was good from the rest of the world; this included industry, medicine, government, education, western alcohol, tableware and, lastly, food – particularly meat.

Many foreigners lived in Yokohama at this time and, of course, they ate European food when possible. They wanted beef so the Japanese built a slaughterhouse in Yokohama in 1865; this was the first example in Japanese history. Cows were obtained from Shina (in China) and *kobe* (*hyogo* prefecture). Gradually butcher's shops were opened in many places but social acceptance was rather slow in coming; Japanese people walking by these shops would close their eyes and pinch their noses until they were out of range.

The first European restaurant was opened in 1866 and the *Meiji* emperor had a European meal for the first time in 1872 on New Year's Day. This was a very signifcant event indeed for cookery in Japan, particularly because New Year's Day is the most important festival in the Japanese calendar and the emperor was certainly making a political statement by eating this meal. Common people began to use European tableware (as well as traditional chopsticks) at this time.

*Sukiyaki* (beef boiled in a pan) became a popular meal – something which would not have been possible without the wider availability of beef. Canned ingredients appeared in 1877 and, in 1925, gas was introduced as a fuel. Refrigerators and thermos flasks became available, the former having an important impact on Japanese cooking partly because of the summer climate. The diet of the common people in Japan improved greatly during this period. The first cookery schools were built, magazines and newspapers offered cookery features and radio stations broadcast programmes about cooking. Cookery training is now taken very seriously in Japan and government licences are required to prepare and sell certain types of food, including the famous semi-poisonous *fugu* (blow fish).

### *Showa* Age (AD 1927–present)

In 1937 the Asian mainland war took place prior to the second world war and this is known as the *Nikkajihen* era. The period of the second world war (1941) is known as *taiheiyo*. The food situation gradually worsened and rationing was introduced. For example, one cup of rice was allowed per person per day and old people or children had less than this; half a white radish every two days was the ration for a five-person family; fish was eaten twice a month and beef only once a month. People ate weeds when possible and there was widespread malnutrition. One judge who had a very strong will tried to live only on his rations, but he died in the attempt. All food was very expensive after the war but many kinds of new ingredients appeared. For as long as ten years after the war rice was still rationed; however most schools had catered for the children's meals.

Automation was slowly being introduced in agriculture and Japan began to import American rice and dried beans. American rice does not have the distinctive taste of the Japanese varieties but it is far more widely available. Where possible American rice is used in this book, but where it is important to use Japanese rice this is noted in the ingredients list.

Many kinds of foreign fruits were cultivated in Japan from about the mid-fifties and this trend is reflected in some of the recipes in this book.

# Japanese Seasonal Festivals

Festivals form an important part of Japanese life and they have special meals associated with them. Some of these dishes are included in this book but many of them are too difficult. The major festivals, known as *Gosekku*, are:

1 *JinJitsu* – 7th January
2 *Joshi* – 3rd March
3 *Tango* – 5th May
4 *Tanabata* – 7th July
5 *Choyo* – 9th September

The *Gosekku* idea came from China where people attached great importance to some numbers and dates. The Japanese tradition started in the *Heian Age* (794–1191) but at this time *Sekku* meant a religious offering. *Gosekku* became national festivals in the *Tokugawa* period during the *Edo Age*, then they went out of public recognition after the *Meiji* period. People still keep these ceremonies privately but the names have been changed:

1 *Nanagusa* (or *Haru No Nanakusa*) – 7th January
2 *Momo No Sekku* (or *Hina Matsuri*) – 3rd March
3 *Shobu No Sekku* (or *Kodomo No Hi*) – 5th May
4 *Tanabata Matsuri* – 7th July
5 *Kiku No Sekku* – 9th September

*Nanagusa*: People eat seven kinds of special vegetables – *nanakusa kayu* – on this festival. If they have this *kayu* on 7th January for breakfast it is believed that they will not become ill during the year!

150 g/5 oz [¾ cup] Japanese or long-grain rice
50 g/2 oz of each of the following plants:
*seri* (Japanese parsley)
*nazuna* (shepherd's purse)
*gogyo*
*hakobera* (chickweed)
*hotokenoza*
*suzuna*
*suzushiro*
½ teaspoon salt

Put the rice in a bowl, partly fill the bowl with cold water, gently stir the grains, then pour off the water and repeat two or three times.

Drain the rice in a sieve or colander for about 30 to 60 minutes. Transfer to a large saucepan which has a lid. Pour in cold water, adding five times the volume of rice. Soak for 2 hours.

Wash, dry and chop the plants. Soak the chopped plants in cold water for 10 minutes, then drain.

Bring the rice to the boil, then reduce the heat to a low setting and put the lid on the pan. Simmer the rice for 40 to 50 minutes. Sprinkle the chopped ingredients and salt into the pan and put the lid back on firmly. Turn off the heat and allow the rice to steam for 5 minutes. Fork the ingredients into the rice, then transfer to small bowls.

*Momo No Sekku*: Once parents have a daughter they celebrate annually with a doll ceremony – *hina ningyo* – on 3rd March. They drink sweet thick *sake* – *ama zake* – to toast their daughter's good health.

*Shobu No Sekku*: Parents with a son also celebrate annually, on 5th May. They make a very big material fish decoration which is placed outside the house. They bathe in an iris leaf bath – *shobu*. For the boy's health they eat *chimaki* – specially prepared sticky rice.

*Tanabata Matsuri*: There is a legend which says that two stars *Kengyu Boshi* and *Shokujo Boshi* met to lay the Milky Way between them on 7th July. There was already a *Kiko Den* star festival (originally adopted from China) celebrated in the *Nara Age* (AD 710–784). Children hope that they will make rapid progress in learning to write the Japanese language, so they write some characters with a brush on a special piece of paper (*Tanzaku*), then rub the paper with an ink stick dipped in the juice of the sweet potato leaf. The papers are then hung on bamboo sticks and thrown in the river on the evening of 7th July.

*Kiku No Sekku*: Chrysanthemum petals are floated on *sake*. The Japanese believe that when you drink this *sake* your life will be long.

# Glossary of Japanese Ingredients and Cookery Terms

**Abura age:** fried soya bean cake.
**Abura age maki:** fried meat with soya bean cake roll.
**Agedango no amazu an kake:** meatballs with vegetables and sauce.
**Agedashi dofu:** fried bean curd.
**Agenasu to butaniku:** fried aubergines [eggplant] and meat.
**Amadai kogane yaki:** grilled [broiled] sea bream.
**Ama zake:** sweet thick rice wine.
**Amazu:** vinegar dressing.
**Amazu an:** sweet vinegar sauce.
**Azuki:** dried red beans (also known as aduki beans).
**Benishoga:** red ginger pickles.
**Butaniku no misodare yaki:** barbecued pork.
**Butaniku no tempura:** fried pork in batter.
**Butaniku to daikon nabe:** pork cooked at the table.
**Chahan:** fried rice with vegetables.
**Chakai:** the tea ceremony.
**Chawan mushi:** steamed egg with meat.
**Chimaki:** special sticky rice.
**Chirashi zushi:** vinegar-flavoured rice (unrolled).
**Daikon:** a large white radish.
**Daikon ba:** the leaves of a large white radish.
**Daikon no gomaabura itame:** fried large white radish.
**Donabe:** a special shallow saucepan.
**Ebi koromo age:** fried cauliflower with prawns [shrimp].
**Fugu:** blow fish, poisonous if not correctly prepared.
**Ganmodoki:** bean curd with vegetables.
**Gyuniku no tataki:** grilled [broiled] beef.
**Gobo to gyuniku no nitsuke:** boiled burdock with beef.
**Go sekku:** the five seasonal festivals.
**Gohan:** rice (usually steamed).
**Gomai oroshi:** a technique for fish preparation.

**Gomame:** dried small fish.
**Gomoku mame:** boiled soya beans.
**Gosei zu:** compound vinegar.
**Gyoza:** fried meat dumplings.
**Gyuniku no maki age:** rolled beef with vegetables.
**Gyuniku no tsukudani:** boiled beef.
**Gyuniku no wakatake yaki:** rolled beef with vegetables, for example green beans.
**Hana renkon:** a flower shape cut from a lotus root.
**Happosai:** fried vegetables and meat.
**Harumaki:** spring roll.
**Harusame:** potato or soya bean starch noodles.
**Hikiniku no ishigaki age:** fried meatballs.
**Hiyayakko:** cold bean curd.
**Hiyamugi:** cold white noodles.
**Hiyashi dori:** chicken salad.
**Hiya zake:** cold rice wine.
**Hon mirin:** a type of sweetened rice wine.
**Hon naoshi:** another type of sweetened rice wine.
**Horenso no ohitashi:** boiled spinach.
**Hosomaki zushi:** a slim roll of vinegar-flavoured rice.
**Ichiya zushi:** vinegar-flavoured rice.
**Ii:** steamed unpolished rice.
**Ika no ring age:** fried squid.
**Ika no teri ni:** boiled squid.
**Imo gohan:** rice with sweet potatoes.
**Inari zushi:** fried soya bean cake with vinegar-flavoured rice.
**Itazuri:** a cooking technique for cucumber.
**Iwashi no agedango:** friend sardine balls.
**Iwashi no fry:** fried sprats.
**Iwashi no Korean style:** boiled sardines with garlic.
**Iwashi no shoga ni:** boiled sardines with ginger.
**Jagaimo no shoga zu:** a type of salad.
**Jagaimo to niku itame:** fried potatoes with meat.
**Joshinko:** a special rice flour.
**Joya nabe:** pork cooked at the table.
**Jozo zu:** brewed vinegar.

11

**Kabocha no kasane age:** fried pumpkin with ham.

**Kaiseki:** a light snack served with the tea ceremony.

**Kaiseki ryori:** a style of meal with which rice wine is served.

**Kake dashi, kake jiru:** two similar stocks.

**Kake mochi:** broken sticky rice cake.

**Kaki age:** fried vegetables.

**Kaki fry:** fried oysters.

**Kaki gohan:** rice with oysters.

**Kaki no dote nabe:** oysters cooked at the table.

**Kakitama jiru:** a thick egg soup.

**Kako zu:** processed vinegar.

**Kampyo:** a dried bottle gourd.

**Kani meshi:** rice with crab.

**Kani no shoga zu:** crab with vinegar dressing.

**Kanitama:** fried egg and crab.

**Kani zushi:** crab with vinegar-flavoured rice.

**Kanten:** a gelatine-type setting agent made from seaweed, similar to agar agar.

**Kan zake:** warm rice wine.

**Kara age:** fried chicken.

**Karei kara age:** fried flounder.

**Katsuobushi:** bonito fish, a member of the tuna family.

**Katsura muki:** a special cutting technique.

**Kawari nyumen:** a hot soup with white noodles.

**Kayaku gohan:** rice with vegetables and chicken.

**Kayu:** rice porridge.

**Kazunoko:** salted herring roe.

**Kiku zake:** rice wine decorated with a few chrysanthemum petals.

**Kikuka kabu:** a chrysanthemum carved from a turnip.

**Kikurage:** dried wooden ear mushrooms.

**Kinshi tamago:** a way of preparing eggs.

**Kirichigai:** a cutting technique used for garnishing ingredients.

**Kohaku kamaboko:** red and white fish cake served for the New Year's Day meal.

**Koikuchi shoyu:** thick soy sauce.

**Kombu:** dried kelp seaweed.

**Konnyaku:** a special cake prepared from a root vegetable similar to yam, known as the devil's tongue plant.

**Kotori no suehiro yaki:** fried minced [ground] chicken.

**Kowameshi:** steamed unpolished rice.

**Kuri gohan:** rice with chestnuts.

**Kuri kinton:** mashed sweet potatoes and chestnuts.

**Kushi dango:** a type of sweet made from sticky rice.

**Kushi katsu:** fried pork kebabs.

**Kyuri no ichiya zuke:** cucumber pickles.

**Kyuri to wakame no sunomono:** cucumber and seaweed with vinegar dressing.

**Maki zushi:** rolled vinegar-flavoured rice.

**Makisu:** a bamboo blind used as a guide for rolling *sushi* or other ingredients.

**Matsuba giri:** a cutting technique.

**Mirin:** sweetened rice wine used for cooking.

**Misago:** a type of edible seabird.

**Miso:** soya bean paste, either white or red.

**Misoshiru:** soya bean paste soup.

**Mitsuba:** Japanese parsley, for garnish.

**Mochi:** sticky rice cake.

**Moyashi no wasabi ae:** bean sprouts with green mustard.

**Moyashi to butaniku ae:** bean sprouts and pork with green mustard.

**Mushi tamago:** steamed egg.

**Mushidori no sauce kake:** steamed chicken with soy sauce dressing.

**Nabe:** cooking at the table.

**Nagashi kan:** a special mould for making bean curd.

**Namasu:** mix raw or grilled [broiled] ingredients with vinegar dressing.

**Nasu no hasami age:** fried aubergines [eggplant] with pork and prawns.

**Nasu to piman no miso itame:** fried aubergines [eggplants] and green peppers.

**Nihai zu:** a type of vinegar dressing.

**Niban dashi:** stock.

**Niboshi:** small dried sardines.

**Niboshi dashi:** a type of stock.

**Nigiri zushi:** small balls of rice with raw fish.

**Nihai zu:** flavoured vinegar.

**Nijimasu no kaori yaki:** fried rainbow trout.

**Nikudango no tamago mabushi:** steamed meatballs.

**Nikujaga:** beef and potatoes cooked in stock.
**Niku no koromo age:** fried beef.
**Niku no tamago tsukeyaki:** fried beef with egg.
**Ninniku zu:** flavoured vinegar.
**Nishime:** boiled vegetables.
**Nori:** dark purple seaweed, dried to make papery sheets.
**Oboro gohan:** rice with meat and vegetables.
**Okonomi yaki:** a pancake [crêpe] made with vegetables and meat.
**Onigiri:** rice balls.
**Oshi zushi:** moulded vinegar-flavoured rice.
**Otoshibuta:** a flat wooden lid (smaller than the pan) put on top of ingredients as they cook to keep them immersed in liquid.
**Oyako donburi:** rice with chicken and egg.
**Ponzu:** processed vinegar.
**Ponzu joyu:** a dipping sauce.
**Renkon no jigatsuo ni:** lotus roots with bonito fish.
**Saba no bou zushi:** mackerel with vinegar-flavoured rice.
**Saba no chukafu miso ni:** mackerel with soya bean paste.
**Saba no Korean style yaki:** grilled [broiled] mackerel.
**Sakanadango no kikuka age:** fried fishballs.
**Sake:** rice wine.
**Sanbai zu:** a vinegar dressing.
**Sanmai oroshi:** a technique for fish preparation.
**Sasami no fry:** fried chicken with almonds.
**Sasami no ham maki:** rolled chicken with ham.
**Sashimi:** raw fish.
**Satoimo:** small, onion-shaped root vegetable. Light grey in colour and similar to potato.
**Sekihan:** rice with red beans.
**Sen roppon:** a cutting technique.
**Sengiri:** a technique used to produce finely cut food.
**Shabu shabu:** beef cooked at the table.
**Shiitake:** dried mushrooms, widely used in Japanese cooking.
**Shio zuke:** salted pickles.
**Shirataki:** noodles made from the dried tubers of the devil's tongue plant.
**Shiratamako:** a type of rice flour.
**Shiro shoyu:** white soy sauce.
**Shochu:** very strong cheap *sake*.
**Shoga amazu zuke:** ginger pickles.
**Shoga yaki:** fried pork with ginger.
**Shokubeni:** red food colouring.
**Shoyu:** soy sauce.
**Shumai:** steamed meat dumplings.
**Soumen:** fine white noodles.
**Su:** rice vinegar.
**Subuta:** fried pork and vegetables with sauce.
**Sukiyaki:** boiled beef and vegetables.
**Sunomono:** salad with vinegar dressing.
**Sushi:** vinegar-flavoured rice.
**Sushi waku:** a mould for vinegar-flavoured rice.
**Takenoko gohan:** rice with bamboo shoots.
**Tako su:** octopus with vinegar dressing.
**Takuan:** large white pickled radishes.
**Tamago dofu:** steamed egg cake.
**Tamago korroke:** egg croquettes.
**Tamago yaki:** egg omelette.
**Tamago zosui:** rice porridge with egg.
**Tamari joyu:** heavy soy sauce.
**Tanabata soumen:** fine white noodles with vegetables.
**Tane:** batter.
**Tanzaku giri:** a cutting technique.
**Taragon zu:** processed vinegar.
**Tare:** a sauce.
**Tazukuri:** boiled small fish served for the New Year's Day meal.
**Tebiraki:** fish preparation technique.
**Tempura (mori awase):** ingredients coated with batter and deep fried.
**Tempura shikishi:** paper used to line dishes for serving deep fried food.
**Tendashi:** a dipping sauce.
**Teppan yaki:** barbecued beef and vegetables.
**Tofu:** bean curd.
**Tokkuri:** a pottery *sake* flask.
**Tonkatsu:** fried pork.
**Toridango no teri ni:** minced [ground] chicken balls.

**Tori no mizutaki:** chicken cooked at the table.
**Tori no tatsuta age:** chicken fritters.
**Tori wasa:** chicken salad.
**Toriniku namba maki:** rolled chicken.
**Toriniku no barei maki:** rolled chicken with potato.
**Tsubuan:** sweet red beans.
**Tsukejiru:** a dipping sauce.
**Tsuke mono:** pickles.
**Udon:** white noodles.
**Umeboshi:** pickled red plums.
**Usukuchi shoyu:** light soy sauce.
**Usuyaki tamago:** a technique used to prepare eggs.
**Wagashi:** sweets.

**Wakame:** dried seaweed.
**Wakatake jiru:** clear bamboo shoot soup.
**Wakatake ni:** boiled bamboo shoots.
**Wan dane:** garnishes used for soup.
**Wappa gohan:** rice with salmon.
**Wari zu:** vinegar sauce.
**Wasabi:** Japanese green mustard vegetable.
**Yakiniku:** barbecued beef.
**Yakisoba:** fried noodles.
**Yakitori:** chicken kebabs.
**Yakiudon:** fried white noodles.
**Yasai itame:** fried vegetables.
**Yose nabe:** seaweed cooked at the table.
**Yu dofu:** bean curd cooked at the table.
**Zenzai:** a sweet soup with red beans.
**Zosui:** rice porridge made with stock.

# A Guide to Using and Storing Japanese Ingredients

Selecting the best ingredients is very important for any type of cooking, especially so for Japanese food. Once selected, many of the ingredients need to be stored carefully to keep them in the best condition.

**Bean Curd** (*tofu*): Mix some water with a pinch of salt in a container. Float the bean curd in the water, seal the container tightly and put it in the refrigerator. The bean curd will keep for one to two weeks but it is best used as fresh as possible.

**Bonito Fish** (*katsuobushi*): Keep in a freezer. It is not necessary to defrost.

**Dried Bottle Gourd** (*kampyo*): Store in an airtight plastic bag, or container, in the refrigerator.

**Dried Chinese Mushrooms** (*shiitake*): Store in an airtight container or plastic bag in the refrigerator.

**Dried Kelp Seaweed** (*kombu*): Store in a tightly sealed container or plastic bag in the refrigerator.

**Dried Purple Seaweed Sheets** (*nori*): Store in a tightly sealed plastic bag in the refrigerator.

**Fresh Root Ginger:** Peel and cut as required, then put it in a plastic bag and freeze. When you use it, you can grate the frozen ginger, defrosting it first.

**Japanese Soy Sauce:** Japanese soy sauce is made from soya beans and wheat to which are added malt and salt. The mixture is then fermented and ripened. There are several different kinds of soy sauce and you can choose the appropriate variety for your recipe; however for this book I will use only thick soy sauce (*koikuchi shoyu*).

When using soy sauce, to retain its full aroma, you should not cook the food for too long after adding the sauce. If you overcook the food at this stage the aroma will disappear and the soy sauce will colour the ingredients too much.

Soy sauce includes salt; this means you can keep it for quite a long time but if it is stored for too long it will become dark in colour and lose its nice flavour and smell. A plastic container of soy sauce should keep for about eighteen months and a glass container should keep for up to two years. Once you open the soy sauce, re-cover it tightly and put it in a cool, dark place.

**Thick Soy Sauce** (*koikuchi shoyu*): This soy sauce constitutes the majority of production and is the most common soy sauce used for cooking in Japan. It has a distinct aroma and it can be used on its own as a dipping sauce. The soy sauce removes the smell from fish and meat, but the high salt content of the sauce causes these ingredients to shrink slightly.

**Light-coloured Soy Sauce** (*usukuchi shoyu*): There is two percent extra salt in this sauce and the ripening time is shorter than for the thick soy sauce. People use this soy sauce mostly as a preservative because it allows the natural colour of food to be retained. This sauce lacks some of the aroma and flavour of the other varieties.

**Heavy Soy Sauce** (*tamari joyu*): This soy sauce is made from soya beans alone and it is made in a similar way to soya bean paste (*miso*). The soya beans are formed into balls and allowed to mature for one year, during which time the soy sauce exudes from the balls. This sauce is very heavy, dark in colour and it has a sweet smell; it can be used as a dipping sauce for raw fish (*sashimi*) or for flavouring food.

**White Soy Sauce** (*shiro shoyu*): This soy sauce is made from a higher percentage of wheat than other types and it matures in a short time. It has a very light colour and a pleasant smell. It can be used when boiling food so that the natural colour of the ingredients is retained. It is used only for cooking.

**Mirin:** Mirin is made by fermenting rice, malt and steamed glutinous rice in alcohol. There is a sweet variety which can be used for a number of dishes as well as for glazing foods. There are several different kinds of mirin which may be used in cooking, or for drinking.

**Hon Mirin:** This *mirin* has been used for a long time for sweetening ingredients and making glazes. It has about 13.5% alcohol.

**Shin Mirin:** There is very little alcohol in this type of *mirin*, which consists of syrup and chemical flavouring. It can be sold in any shop in Japan in contrast to *Hon Mirin* which can only be sold in licensed shops.

**Hon Naoshi:** This *mirin* is suitable for drinking – known as *naoshi mirin* or *ryuin*. It is made by adding plenty of cheap spirits (*shochu*) to *mirin* and leaving it to mature for about 10 days. This is not a sophisticated drink and it should not be served at dinner.

*Mirin* creates a special flavour and aroma in food and it is a very important ingredient for Japanese cookery. However, because *mirin* contains alcohol it can make meat tough and it can alter the taste of some ingredients. If this is a problem you can use *nikiri mirin* which is made by bringing *mirin* to the boil to remove the alcohol.

When *mirin* is used with soy sauce for glazing a surface, the reduced sugar in the *mirin* and the amino acids in the soy sauce react to make *meranoijin*. It is sometimes possible to use ordinary sugar instead of *mirin* but cane sugar is not the same as reduced sugar and the reaction is much slower, so cane sugar may not be suitable for some recipes.

**Rice Vinegar** (*su*): There are several different kinds of vinegar.

**Brewed Vinegar** (*jozo zu*): This is made using vinegar acid fungi, alcohol and sugar. Typical vinegars are *kome zu* (more mature *sake*), alcohol *zu*, *bakuga zu* and *ringo zu*.

**Compound Vinegar** (*gosei zu*): This vinegar is made from water and *hyozu san* which is produced by reacting wood or lime with salt, seasoning and colour material. This vinegar has a sharp acid smell.

**Processed Vinegar** (*kako zu*): This vinegar has added flavouring and it is really a form of instant food. Examples are *ponzu*, *nihai zu*, *sanbai zu*, *taragon zu* and *ninniku zu*.

Brewed vinegar is far superior to compound vinegar in many ways, particularly for flavour, aroma and permeation characteristics. Compound vinegar is cheaper than brewed vinegar but you should not use it for cookery.

Vinegar has an antiseptic action, and you can keep it for quite a long time but after opening a bottle the vinegar can sometimes become muddy. When vinegar is kept in the sun, the flavour and smell will disappear, so store it in a cool, dark place.

**Sake:** Sake is a very important ingredient in Japanese cooking. There are two varieties: brewed and synthetic. Brewed, mature sake has a flavour and aroma that is missing in the synthetic type and when you use the synthetic type for cooking it will produce a quite different flavour. Once you open a bottle of sake you should use it as soon as possible and reseal the bottle tightly meanwhile, keeping it in a cool dark place. In addition to its culinary use, there are many ways of serving sake but normally it is drunk straight, either warm or cold. Heated sake is the traditional drink and does taste different. To warm *sake* – known as (*kan zake*) – put some of the sake in a pottery flask (*tokkuri*), heat it in a water bath to about 50 C/120 F.

**Soya Bean Paste (*Miso*):** Soya bean paste was imported from China in the *Yamato* age (about AD 400–500) and was adopted by the Japanese people; eventually *miso* cookery became uniquely Japanese. There are many kinds of soya bean paste and each one has a slightly different flavour, smell and colour. Japanese people created about one hundred different varieties which were suited to local geography, weather, tastes and ingredients. The paste can be either white or red, smooth or coarse.

Soya bean paste contributes a special flavour and smell to dishes, it removes the smell from fish and meat and the paste absorbs oil. Store in an airtight container away from the sun. Smooth the surface of the paste flat after use. you should not store the paste near anything which has a strong smell.

**Sticky Rice Cake (*mochi*):** Put the rice cake in a plastic bag and freeze for several months.

## Creating Authentic Flavour

It is not possible to reproduce a delicate flavour simply by using accurate measurements. Timing is very important; there are different timing requirements for each type of cooking technique. For example, it is possible to lose a delicate flavour by marinating food for too short a period of time; or the flavour can be destroyed by overboiling the food.

Seasoning is intended to add flavour to ingredients but it can also serve other purposes, such as producing an aroma or acting as a preservative in certain dishes. If you put too much sugar or acid in food you can correct the flavour to some extent by using an opposite seasoning. If you put too much salt into food, you can only counteract this by adding water so you should be very careful when adding salt. Add only eighty percent of the required amount of salt initially, add all the other seasoning ingredients, then test the flavour; finally, if you need to add extra salt you can do this carefully and remain in control of the result.

When you cook with sugar and salt, you should add the sugar first. When the sugar flavour has percolated through the ingredients, add the salt. If you put the salt in first, the sugar flavour will not penetrate through the ingredients. You can remember the correct order of seasoning with this rhyme which is based on the way Japanese children learn characters:

Sa (*sato*) sugar
Shi (*shio*) salt
Su (*su*) vinegar
Se (*shoyu*) soy sauce
So (*miso*) soya bean paste
(*SA SHI SU SE SO*)

Try to check the flavour of a dish just once. If you taste the food a few times, leave a little time between the tests, otherwise your tongue will lose sensitivity. Try to achieve a flavour slightly weaker than you ultimately require, because when the food cools as it is served the flavour will appear stronger.

# Shiru Mono

## —— *Soups* ——

Japanese soup is a very important appetiser, particularly with *sashimi* and *yaki mono* (seafood). There are two types of soup, one is *suimono* (clear soup) and the other one is *misoshiru*. *Dashi* (soup stock) for Japanese cookery is very different from Western and Chinese stocks. *Dashi* is prepared very quickly to achieve a nice smell and flavour, and if you cook it too long the *dashi* will become too strong. *Suimono* (clear soup) is flavoured with salt and a little soy sauce to give a good smell and colour. Do not cook the soup too long or add too much flavouring. *Misoshiru* should not be boiled too long after the *miso* is added to the dashi.

## **Misoshiru**

### —— *Soya Bean Paste Soup* ——

(Illustrated on pages 166/167)

| METRIC/IMPERIAL | AMERICAN |
|---|---|
| 75–90 g/3–3½ oz white, red or mixed *miso* | 3–3½ oz white, red or mixed *miso* |
| 1 litre/1¾ pints soup stock (page 18) | 1 quart soup stock (page 18) |
| 2 spring onions to garnish | 2 scallions for garnish |

First prepare the spring onion [scallions] for garnishing the soup: trim off the roots and any bruised leaves, then wash and chop them finely. Set aside.

Put the *miso* in a small bowl and add some of the stock. Mix the stock and *miso* until smooth. Pour the remaining stock into a saucepan and add the *miso* mixture. Bring to the boil and immediately turn off the heat – do not cook the soup too long otherwise it will lose its flavour and fragrance. Serve, garnished with the chopped spring onions [scallions]. **Serves 4**

**Note:** other ingredients can be added to *Misoshiru*. For example, 1-cm/½-in cubes of *tofu* or vegetables can be stirred into the soup. Trim or peel vegetables – large white radish, cabbage, onion or potatoes, for example – then cut them into very fine strips – *sengiri* style (see page 163). *Wakame* (seaweed), cut into 1.5-cm/¾-in wide strips, or beaten egg can also be added. Add ingredients with the paste mixture. *Tofu* and potato take a little longer, so boil gently until the *tofu* floats and the potato is tender.

# Soup Stock

### Method 1

| METRIC/IMPERIAL | AMERICAN |
|---|---|
| 12–15 *niboshi* | 12–15 *niboshi* |

Cut the heads off the *niboshi* and clean out the inside of the fish. If they are not cleaned the stock will become cloudy and slightly bitter. Pour 1 litre/1¾ pints [1 quart] water into a saucepan. Place the *niboshi* in a large metal sieve in the pan, resting it on the rim so it is partly submerged. Bring slowly to the boil over a low to moderate heat, then immediately turn off the heat. Leave to soak for 30 minutes then discard the fish.

### Method 2

| METRIC/IMPERIAL | AMERICAN |
|---|---|
| 10-cm/4-in square *kombu* | 4-in square *kombu* |
| 5 g/¼ oz dried bonito fish | ¼ oz dried bonito fish |

Wipe the kelp with a piece of absorbent kitchen paper and make cuts three-quarters of the way through the kelp in a number of places. Put the kelp in a saucepan with 1 litre/1¾ pints [1 quart] water. Bring to the boil over a low to moderate heat and add the bonito fish, then immediately turn off the heat. Leave the stock for 30 minutes, then strain it through a sieve.

**Note:** there are several instant *dashi* stock powders available. Follow the instructions on the packet to make these.

# Suimono

—— *Clear Soup* ——

(Illustrated on page 25)

| METRIC/IMPERIAL | AMERICAN |
|---|---|
| 1 litre/1¾ pints *dashi* (page 153) | 1 quart *dashi* (page 153) |
| salt | salt |
| 2 teaspoons Japanese soy sauce | 2 teaspoons Japanese soy sauce |

Bring the *dashi* to the boil with 1 teaspoon salt and the soy sauce, then serve with any one of the following garnishes. I give four different examples of *wan dane* garnish. You should choose one which is appropriate to the season and to your taste. **Serves 4**

# Wan Dane 1

—— *Soup Garnish 1* ——

(Illustrated on page 25)

METRIC/IMPERIAL

300 g/11 oz peeled cooked prawns or shrimps (if you can obtain uncooked prawns, then peel them and use them in preference to pre-cooked shellfish)

1 egg

2 tablespoons cornflour

salt

3-cm/1¼-in piece cucumber

½ tomato (cut in half vertically)

piece of fresh lemon peel 1.5 cm/¾ in wide and 3 cm/¼ in long

AMERICAN

¾ lb peeled cooked shrimps (if you can obtain raw shrimps, then peel them and use them in preference to cooked shrimp)

1 egg

2 tablespoons cornstarch

salt

1¼-in piece cucumber

½ tomato (cut in half vertically)

piece of fresh lemon peel ¾-in wide and ¼-in long

If you are using uncooked prawns [shrimp], add them to a pan of boiling salted water, bring back to the boil, then drain the prawns [shrimp]. Toss them in a sieve to remove the last of the water. Beat the egg thoroughly. Mince [grind] the prawns [shrimp] finely, then mix them with the beaten egg, the cornflour [cornstarch] and a generous ½ teaspoon salt in a bowl.

Bring a small saucepan of water to the boil. Make small balls from the prawn [shrimp] mixture – they should be about 2 cm/¾ in. in diameter. Lower the balls into the boiling water and cook until they float to the surface. Drain the balls in a sieve.

Using the handle of a small spoon, scoop out the inside of the cucumber to make a hole measuring about 1 cm/½ in. in diameter. Peel the cucumber following the *katsura muki* technique (see page 164), then cut it into 2-mm/1/10-in thick slices.

Cut the tomato half into four wedges and remove the seeds, then peel two-thirds of each wedge from the top, leaving the skin peeled back decoratively on the tomato. Cut the lemon peel into 1.5-cm/¾-in long, very fine sticks.

Arrange all the garnishing ingredients, except the lemon peel sticks, in an attractive pattern in small individual bowls. Pour the hot soup gently into the bowls, then float the lemon sticks in the middle of the soup. **Serves 4**

# Wan Dane 2

—— *Soup Garnish 2* ——

| METRIC/IMPERIAL | AMERICAN |
|---|---|
| 1 medium squid | 1 medium-size squid |
| 4 whole uncooked Mediterranean prawns | 4 raw jumbo shrimps |
| 2 tablespoons *sake* | 2 tablespoons *sake* |
| 1 tablespoon dried *wakame* | 1 tablespoon dried *wakame* |
| salt | salt |

Prepare the squid following the instructions for method 2 (see page 00), then cut it crossways into 5-mm/$\frac{1}{4}$-in wide pieces. Put the squid into boiling salted water, bring back to the boil, then cook until the squid floats to the surface. Drain the squid in a sieve.

Remove the shells from the prawns [shrimp], leaving their tails on. Using a cocktail stick, remove the veins. Put the prawns [shrimp] in a small saucepan, then add the *sake*, salt and 2 tablespoons water. Bring to the boil. Reduce to a low heat, put a lid on the pan and simmer for 1$\frac{1}{2}$ to 2 minutes so that the prawns [shrimp] are just cooked through. Remove from the heat, take the lid off the pan and leave to cool.

Soak the *wakame* in water for 5 to 10 minutes. When the *wakame* has expanded, cut it into 2-cm/$\frac{3}{4}$-in squares. Put these squares in boiling water, then immediately drain them and toss them in a sieve to remove the last of the water.

Arrange all the ingredients attractively in small individual bowls, then pour the hot soup gently into the bowls. **Serves 4**

# Wan Dane 3

—— *Soup Garnish 3* ——

(Illustrated on page 25)

| METRIC/IMPERIAL | AMERICAN |
|---|---|
| 100 g/4 oz *tofu* | *tofu* |
| $\frac{1}{4}$ pack of mustard and cress | small bunch of garden cress |

Cut the *tofu* into eight pieces. Snip the cress from its bed and put it in a sieve, then rinse thoroughly in water, removing any seed husks which remain.

Put the *tofu* in the soup, bring to the boil and boil gently until the pieces float to the surface. Serve the soup with the *tofu* in small individual bowls and float the cress on top. **Serves 4**

# Wan Dane 4

—— *Soup Garnish 4* ——

| METRIC/IMPERIAL | AMERICAN |
|---|---|
| 100 g/4 oz haddock fillet (select small fillets) | $\frac{1}{4}$ lb haddock fillet (select small fillets) |
| salt and pepper | salt and pepper |
| $\frac{1}{2}$ beaten egg | $\frac{1}{2}$ beaten egg |
| 3-cm/$1\frac{1}{4}$-in piece cucumber | $1\frac{1}{4}$-in piece cucumber |
| cornflour for coating | cornstarch for coating |

Remove the skin and bones from the haddock, then cut the fillets crossways into 3-cm/$1\frac{1}{4}$-in wide pieces. Sprinkle with salt and pepper on both sides and set aside for 10 minutes.

Prepare the beaten egg following the *kinshi tamago* technique (see page 156).

Using the handle of a small spoon, scoop out the inside of the cucumber, making a 1-cm/$\frac{1}{2}$-in diameter hole. Peel the cucumber following the *katsura muki* technique (see page 164) and cut it into 2-mm/$\frac{1}{10}$-in thick slices.

Coat the fish pieces with cornflour [cornstarch], shaking off any excess. Lower them into boiling water and bring back to the boil. Boil gently until the fish floats to the surface and is cooked through. Lift the pieces out with a draining spoon.

Arrange all the ingredients in small individual bowls, then pour the hot soup gently over them. **Serves 4**

# Gohan Mono

## —— *Steamed Rice Dishes* ——

In Japan, rice is an important staple food and since the second world war Japanese people eat polished rice every day. Nowadays young people eat Western meals but rice is still the staple food.

There are many forms of steamed rice used in dishes such as *takikomi gohan, donburi mono, ochazuke, onigiri, zosui, kayu* and *sushi.*

There are a few points to remember when steaming rice. You have to wash the rice about 30–60 minutes before cooking, then leave it to drain in a sieve or colander.

When you steam rice, leave the rice in a tightly covered pan for 5 to 10 minutes (flavoured rice for 15 to 20 minutes) after cooking. This method removes excess water from the cooked rice. The rice should not be left for more than 20 minutes, otherwise it becomes too watery due to condensation from the lid.

After fluffing up the rice, put a clean cloth or a kitchen towel between the lid and the saucepan to absorb condensation until the rice is served.

# Gohan

*—— Steamed Rice ——*

(Illustrated on page 165)

| METRIC/IMPERIAL | AMERICAN |
|---|---|
| 425 g/15 oz Japanese rice or long-grain rice | 2¼ cups Japanese rice or long-grain rice |
| 750 ml/1¼ pints water | 3 cups water |

Wash the rice in a bowl with cold running water: partly fill the bowl with water and stir the rice gently. Pour off the water and repeat two or three times. Drain the rice in a sieve or colander, leaving it for about 30 to 60 minutes. This allows time for the rice to absorb some water and to partially soften the grains.

Put the rice in a heavy-based saucepan which has a tight-fitting lid and add the measured water. Cover the saucepan, then bring to the boil over the maximum heat and wait until steam begins to appear around the edge of the lid. Lower the heat and simmer the rice gently for 12 to 13 minutes, keeping the lid tightly on the pan all the time. Increase the heat to the maximum available and cook the rice for a further 10 seconds, then remove the saucepan from the heat. If you are cooking on an electric stove it is very important to use the maximum setting and to allow the ring to reach its maximum heat before timing the 10 seconds. Leave the saucepan, off the heat, with the lid still firmly on top for about 5 to 10 minutes.

Remove the lid and fluff up the rice with a wooden spoon or serving spoon. Wrap a clean linen-towel around the lid, then replace it on the pan so that the towel lies between the lid and the saucepan; it will absorb any steam and prevent condensation forming on the lid. Serve the rice hot in small individual bowls. **Serves 4**

**Note:** If you want to cook a smaller or greater amount of rice, the quantity of water used should always be twenty percent greater than the dry rice, measured in cupfuls.

# Wappa Gohan

—— *Rice with Salmon* ——

(Illustrated on page 28)

| METRIC/IMPERIAL | AMERICAN |
|---|---|
| 425 g/15 oz Japanese rice | $2\frac{1}{4}$ cups Japanese rice |
| 225 g/8 oz fresh salmon | $\frac{1}{2}$ lb fresh salmon |
| 3 tablespoons *sake* | 3 tablespoons *sake* |
| salt | salt |
| *Garnish* | *Garnish* |
| 2-cm/$\frac{3}{4}$-in cube fresh root ginger | $\frac{3}{4}$-in cube fresh ginger root |
| 10-cm/4-in square *nori* | 4-in square *nori* |

Wash the rice in a bowl with cold running water. Partly fill the bowl with water, stir the rice gently, pour off the water and repeat two or three more times. Drain the rice in a sieve or colander for about 30 to 60 minutes. This allows time for the rice to absorb some water and to partially soften.

Meanwhile, prepare the garnish: cut the ginger into thin slices with the grain, then cut each slice into many thin sticks. Soak the prepared ginger in water for 1 to 2 minutes, then drain the sticks in a sieve. Cut the *nori* into 2.5-cm/1-in long strips, then into very fine pieces – about 2 mm/$\frac{1}{10}$ in wide.

Lower the salmon into gently boiling water, bring back to the boil and simmer for 1 minute. Carefully lift the salmon from the water. Remove and discard the bone and skin, then cut the salmon into 2-cm/$\frac{3}{4}$-in cubes. Put these in a heavy-based saucepan which has a tight-fitting lid. Mix the *sake* and $1\frac{1}{2}$ teaspoons salt in a measuring jug, then add enough water to give 750 ml/$1\frac{1}{4}$ pints [3 cups]. Pour this into the saucepan and add the rice.

Cover the pan, then bring to the boil over maximum heat and wait until the steam begins to appear round the edge of the lid. Lower the heat and simmer the rice gently for 12 to 13 minutes, keeping the lid tightly sealed. Increase the heat to the maximum and cook for a further 10 seconds. (If you are cooking on an electric hob [stove], wait until the maximum temperature is reached before timing the 10 seconds.) Leave with the lid on for about 10 to 15 minutes. Remove the lid then fluff up the rice. Wrap a clean tea-towel [linen towel] around the lid, then replace it on the pan until you are ready to serve the rice. Serve the rice hot in small individual bowls and put some ginger on each portion. Garnish with *nori*. **Serves 4**

**Opposite page** *Suimono (page 18) with Wan Dane 1 (top) and Wane Dane 3 (bottom)* **Overleaf** *Clockwise from the top: Chirashi Zushi (page 32), Maki Zushi (page 30) and Oshi Zushi (page 34)*

# Kani Zushi

—— *Crab Sushi* ——

(Illustrated opposite)

| METRIC/IMPERIAL | AMERICAN |
|---|---|
| 6 dried *shiitake* | 6 dried *shiitake* |
| 1½ tablespoons sugar | 1½ tablespoons sugar |
| 7½ teaspoons Japanese soy sauce | 7½ teaspoons Japanese soy sauce |
| *Sushi Meshi* prepared from | *Sushi Meshi* prepared from 2¼ cups |
| 425 g/15 oz Japanese rice or long- | Japanese rice or long-grain |
| grain rice (page 154) | rice (page 154) |
| *Garnish* | *Garnish* |
| 4 eggs | 4 eggs |
| 50 g/2 oz shelled peas | ½ cup shelled peas |
| *Shoga Amazu Zuke* (page 138) | *Shoga Amazu Zuke* (page 138) |
| 1 (250-g/8¾-oz) can crab meat | 1 (8-oz) can crabmeat |

Soak the *shiitake* in warm water for 20 minutes, remove and discard the stems, then lightly squeeze the caps. Slice these thinly. Put the *shiitake*, sugar and 100 ml/4 fl oz [½ cup] water in a saucepan, bring to the boil and add the soy sauce. Boil over a low to moderate heat until most of the water has evaporated.

For the garnish: prepare the eggs following the *kinshi tamago* technique (see page 156). Add the peas to boiling salted water, bring back to the boil, then boil for 2 minutes. Remove from the heat and trickle cold water into the pan until the peas become cool. This method of cooling the vegetables avoids wrinkled skins. Slice the *Shoga Amazu Zuke* (ginger pickles) thinly with the grain.

Make the *Sushi Meshi*, using 750 ml/1¼ pints [3 cups] water, following the recipe instructions. Add the *shiitake* to the warm rice and fluff up the grains. You should mix ingredients into warm rice because the flavour will spread through the rice evenly. Spread the rice out on a big deep plate. Decorate the *sushi* attractively with the eggs, crab, *Shoga Amazu Zuke* and drained peas, then serve cold. Each person should help themselves, transferring the *sushi* on to individual plates. **Serves 4**

*Top: Wappa Gohan (page 24); bottom: Kani Zushi*

# Maki Zushi

—— *Rolled Sushi* ——

(Illustrated on pages 26/27)

METRIC/IMPERIAL
*Sushi Meshi* prepared from
425 g/15 oz Japanese rice (page 154)
4 sheets *nori*
2 eggs
3 tablespoons plus 1 teaspoon sugar
salt
1 tablespoon oil
20 g/$\frac{3}{4}$ oz *kampyo*
1 tablespoon *mirin* or *sake*
3 dried *shiitake*
4$\frac{1}{2}$ teaspoons Japanese soy sauce
225 g/8 oz peeled cooked prawns or
shrimps
3 or 4 drops *shokubeni* (Japanese red
food colouring) mixed with 1
tablespoon water
100 ml/4 fl oz rice vinegar
20-cm/8-in piece halved cucumber
(cut lengthways into thin strips)
*Shoga Amazu Zuke* (page 138) to
garnish

AMERICAN
*Sushi Meshi* prepared from 2$\frac{1}{4}$ cups
Japanese rice (page 154)
4 sheets *nori*
2 eggs
3 tablespoons plus 1 teaspoon sugar
salt
1 tablespoon oil
$\frac{3}{4}$ oz *kampyo*
1 tablespoon *mirin* or *sake*
3 dried *shiitake*
4$\frac{1}{2}$ teaspoons Japanese soy sauce
$\frac{1}{2}$ lb peeled cooked shrimps
3 or 4 drops *shokubeni* (Japanese red
food coloring) mixed with 1
tablespoon water
$\frac{1}{2}$ cup rice vinegar
8-in piece halved cucumber (cut
lengthwise into thin strips)
*Shoga Amazu Zuke* (page 138) to
garnish

Prepare the *Sushi Meshi* following the recipe instructions. Place two sheets of *nori* together with the shiny sides in. Pick them up at one end, holding the sheets together, and wave them above a gas or electric ring [burner] for a few moments until they become light green. Take care not to burn yourself; if your hand feels too hot you are too close to the heat – about 13 cm/5 in away is correct. Repeat the process for the remaining two sheets of nori.

Beat the eggs thoroughly with 2 teaspoons of the sugar and a pinch of salt. Heat a frying pan, pour in the oil and wipe it around the pan with a pad of absorbent kitchen paper to grease the surface evenly. Reduce the heat to a moderate setting and pour the eggs into the pan. Tilt the pan until the eggs cover the base [bottom] evenly then allow them to set. Turn the eggs over and fry for few seconds on the other side. Cut the cooked eggs into 1-cm/$\frac{1}{2}$-in wide strips.

Wash the *kampyo* in plenty of water. Pour off the water and squeeze the *kampyo* in the bowl. Sprinkle 2 tablespoons salt over the *kampyo* and crumple it with both hands for 5 minutes. Rinse the *kampyo* and drain thoroughly. Bring a saucepan of water to the boil, add the *kampyo* and bring back to the boil. Simmer gently for 4 to 5 minutes. Reserve 8 tablespoons of the cooking liquid, then drain the *kampyo* in a sieve or colander and allow to cool.

Mix the *kampyo* with the reserved cooking liquid, 2 tablespoons of the sugar and the *mirin* or *sake* in a saucepan and bring to the boil. Simmer gently until most of the water has evaporated, stirring carefully. Leave to cool. Cut the *kampyo* into pieces measuring about 20 cm/8 in long.

Soak the *shiitake* in warm water for 20 minutes, remove and discard the stems and lightly squeeze out the mushroom caps. Thinly slice the squeezed out mushrooms. Put the slices in a saucepan. Add remaining 2 teaspoons sugar and 3 tablespoons water then bring to the boil. Add the soy sauce, then boil over a low to moderate heat until most of the water has evaporated, stirring well.

Put the prawns [shrimp] in boiling salted water, bring back to the boil, then boil for 1 minute. Drain the prawns [shrimp] and toss them in a sieve to remove the last of the water. Mince [grind] the prawns [shrimp] finely. Put the prawns [shrimp] in a saucepan then add $\frac{1}{2}$ teaspoon salt and the *shokubeni*. Fry over a low heat, stirring well with three or four chopsticks, until the prawns [shrimp] become dry.

Pour 100 ml/4 fl oz [$\frac{1}{2}$ cup] water into a small bowl and add the rice vinegar. Use this mixture to dampen your hands; try to keep your hands just slightly moist, if they are too wet, as you handle the rice it will become too damp and the *sushi* will not hold its shape correctly.

Lay out a *makisu* (bamboo blind) with the strands of wood running from left to right. Lay one sheet of the *nori* widthways on the bamboo blind. Dampen your hands, take about 175 g/6 oz of the rice, put it on the nori and spread it evenly over the nearest three-quarters of the sheet.

Arrange 2 or 3 strips of egg widthways on the middle of the rice, then add a quarter each of the *kampyo*, prawns [shrimp], cucumber and the *shiitake*. Keep the ingredients neat and close together. Using the bamboo blind as a guide, roll the rice tightly. Carefully unroll the blind and remove the food. Leave the *sushi* with the seamed edge downwards for about 10 minutes to allow it to settle down. Cover the prepared *sushi* with a damp cloth while you are rolling the remaining ingredients; do not allow it to dry out. Repeat using all the remaining ingredients.

Prepare a folded damp cloth for wiping the knife, then cut the *sushi* into 8 to 10 slices with a sharp straight-edged knife. Wipe the knife with the damp cloth after each cut. Arrange the *sushi* attractively on individual plates and garnish with some of the ginger pickles. **Serves 4**

**Note:** if preferred, the *sushi* can be garnished with whole cooked prawns.

# Chirashi Zushi

—— *Unrolled Sushi* ——

(Illustrated on pages 26/27)

| METRIC/IMPERIAL | AMERICAN |
|---|---|
| 20 g/¾ oz *kampyo* | ¾ oz *kampyo* |
| salt | salt |
| 5 tablespoons plus 2 teaspoons sugar | 5 tablespoons plus 2 teaspoons sugar |
| 1 tablespoon *mirin* or *sake* | 1 tablespoon *mirin* or *sake* |
| 4 dried *shiitake* | 4 dried *shiitake* |
| 5 tablespoons plus 1½ teaspoons Japanese soy sauce | 5 tablespoons plus 1½ teaspoons Japanese soy sauce |
| 1 medium carrot | 1 medium-size carrot |
| 4 eggs | 4 eggs |
| 100 g/4 oz peeled cooked prawns | ¼ lb peeled cooked prawns |
| 1 (99-g/3½-oz) can tuna, drained | 1 (3-oz) can tuna, drained |
| 50 g/2 oz mange-tout peas or shelled peas | ½ cup snow or sugar peas, or shelled green peas |
| *Sushi Meshi* prepared from 425 g/15 oz Japanese rice (page 154) | *Sushi Meshi* prepared from 2¼ cups Japanese rice (page 154) |

Wash the *kampyo* in plenty of water. Pour off the water and squeeze the *kampyo* in the bowl. Sprinkle 2 tablespoons salt over the *kampyo* and crumple it with both hands for 5 minutes. Rinse and drain the *kampyo*.

Bring a saucepan of water to the boil. Add the *kampyo*, bring back to the boil, and simmer gently for 4 to 5 minutes. Keep 8 tablespoons of the cooking liquid, then drain the *kampyo* in a sieve or colander and allow to cool. Put the *kampyo*, reserved cooking juice, 2 tablespoons of the sugar and the *mirin* or *sake* in a saucepan; bring to the boil. Lightly simmer the mixture until most of the water has evaporated, stirring gently. Leave to cool. Cut the *kampyo* into pieces 5-mm/¼-in wide pieces.

Soak the dried *shiitake* in warm water for 20 minutes, remove and discard their stalks and lightly squeeze the caps. Thinly slice these. Put the *shiitake*, 2 teaspoons of the sugar and 3 tablespoons water in a saucepan, then bring to the boil. Add 4½ teaspoons of the soy sauce, then boil over a low to moderate heat until most of the water has evaporated, stirring well.

Cut the carrot into very fine strips – *sengiri* style (see page 163) – put the carrot, 1 tablespoon of sugar and 100 ml/4 fl oz [½ cup] water in a saucepan and bring to the boil. Add 2 tablespoons of the soy sauce, then boil over a low to moderate heat until most of the water has evaporated, stirring well all the time.

Prepare the eggs following the *kinshi tamago* technique (see page 156). Lower the prawns [shrimp] into a saucepan of boiling salted water, bring back to the boil, then boil for 1 minute. Drain the prawns [shrimp] thoroughly and toss them gently in a sieve to remove the last of the water. It is important that the shellfish are well drained but take care not to damage them as you shake the sieve.

Place the tuna in a small saucepan. Add the remaining sugar and soy sauce, 2 tablespoons water and a pinch of salt, then bring to the boil over a low to moderate heat and boil until most of the water has evaporated, stirring well.

**Note:** presentation plays an important part in Japanese cookery. To ensure that the dish will look its best, follow the preparation instructions carefully. For example, in the above recipe the peas are cooked and cooled following a particular method which is important to give good results. Always arrange the ingredients neatly and serve the dish freshly cooked. Unrolled sushi is easy to prepare and present, so it is a good dish on which to practise your garnishing skills.

Discard the stalks and strings from the mange-tout [snow] peas. Put them in a saucepan of boiling salted water, bring back to the boil, then boil for 1 minute. Drain and immerse the peas in cold water to cool. Drain and toss in a sieve to remove the last of the water. If you are using the green peas, cook them in boiling salted water for 2 minutes. Remove from the heat and trickle cold water into the pan until the peas become cool. This method of cooling the peas avoids wrinkled skins.

Make the *Sushi Meshi*, using 750 ml/1¼ pints [3 cups] water, following the recipe instructions. Add the *kampyo*, *shiitake*, carrot and tuna to the warm rice. You should mix the ingredients into the warm rice because the flavour will spread through the grains evenly. Fluff up the rice, mixing it with the other ingredients. Spread the rice on a big deep plate, then garnish the mixture attractively by arranging the eggs, prawns [shrimp] and mange-tout [snow] peas or green peas on top.

Serve the *sushi* cold; each person should help themselves, transferring a little of the *chirashi zushi* on to individual plates to eat. **Serves 4**

# Oshi Zushi

—— *Moulded Sushi* ——

(Illustrated on pages 26/27)

METRIC/IMPERIAL
*Sushi Meshi* prepared from
425 g/15 oz Japanese rice
100 ml/4 fl oz rice vinegar
2 roll mops (about 75–90 g/3–3½ oz
each)
100 g/4 oz smoked salmon
*Shoga Amazu Zuke* (page 138) to
garnish

AMERICAN
*Sushi Meshi* prepared from 2¼ cups
Japanese rice
½ cup rice vinegar
2 pickled herring fillets (about
3–3½ oz each)
¼ lb smoked salmon
*Shoga Amazu Zuke* (page 138) to
garnish

Make the *Sushi Meshi*, using 750 ml/1¼ pints [3 cups] water, following the recipe instructions. Soak a *sushi waku* (a *sushi* mould) in water for 10 minutes, drain the mould and wipe away any excess water. Pour 100 ml/4 fl oz [½ cup] water and the rice vinegar into a small bowl. Dampen your hands with this mixture. Try to keep your hands lightly moistened. If they are too wet the rice will become too damp and the *sushi* will not hold its shape correctly.

Put the base of the mould inside the outer frame. Cut the roll mops [herrings] in half lengthways. Put these fillets in the mould with the skin underneath. Separate 160–175 g/5½–6 oz of the *Sushi Meshi* and form it into two balls. Put the balls on top of the roll mops [herrings], then spread the rice evenly in the mould. Put the lid on top, then push the lid with both hands applying even pressure for about 1 minute. Remove the frame from the *sushi waku*, then gently lift off the top and bottom of the mould. Remove any odd grains of rice and dampen the mould before making the second batch.

Repeat this process using the smoked salmon instead of the roll mops [herrings]. Cut the salmon into pieces about 1 cm/½ in bigger than the bottom of the mould before pressing the *sushi*.

Prepare a folded damp cloth for wiping the knife. Using a sharp, straight-edged knife, cut the *sushi* widthways into eight pieces. Arrange the two types of *sushi* on individual plates, adding the ginger pickles as a garnish around the edges of the plates. **Serves 4**

# Takenoko Gohan

—— *Rice with Bamboo Shoots* ——

METRIC/IMPERIAL
425 g/15 oz Japanese rice
150 g/5 oz canned bamboo shoots,
drained
1 chicken leg joint
3 tablespoons *sake*
3 tablespoons Japanese soy sauce
3 spring onions to garnish

AMERICAN
2¼ cups Japanese rice
1 (8-oz) can bamboo shoots, drained
1 chicken leg-with-thigh
3 tablespoons *sake*
3 tablespoons Japanese soy sauce
3 scallions for garnish

Wash the rice in a bowl with cold running water. Partly fill the bowl with water, stir the rice gently, then pour off the water and repeat two or three more times. Drain the rice in a sieve or colander for about 30 to 60 minutes; this allows time for the rice to absorb some water and to partially soften the grains.

Cut the bamboo shoots into pieces measuring 1.5 cm/¾ in long and 5 mm/¼ in wide. Prepare the chicken following the instructions on page 159. Remove the skin from the chicken leg, then cut the meat into 1-cm/½-in cubes. Marinate the chicken meat in 1 tablespoon of the *sake* and 1 tablespoon of the soy sauce for 10 minutes.

Put the bamboo shoots, chicken and rice water in a heavy-based saucepan which has a lid. Put the remaining *sake* and soy sauce in a measuring jug, then make up to 750 ml/1¼ pints [3 cups] with water. Pour this into the saucepan. Cover the saucepan, then bring to the boil over the maximum heat and wait until the steam begins to appear around the edge of the lid. Lower the heat and simmer the rice gently for 12 to 13 minutes, keeping the lid tightly on the pan all the time. Increase the heat to the maximum available and cook the rice for a further 10 seconds, then remove the pan from the heat. Leave the saucepan with the lid on for about 10 to 15 minutes (flavoured rice should be left in a sealed pan longer than steamed rice).

Trim the spring onions [scallions] of roots and any bruised leaves, then chop them. Remove the lid from the pan, add the chopped spring onions [scallions], then fluff up the rice with a wooden spoon or serving spoon. Wrap a clean tea-towel [linen towel] around the lid, replace it so that the towel is between the lid and the saucepan until you are ready to serve the rice. Serve the rice hot, in small individual bowls. **Serves 4**

**Note:** you should always use Japanese rice for flavoured-rice recipes.

# Inari Zushi

—— *Fried Soya Bean Cake with Sushi Rice* ——

METRIC/IMPERIAL
8 *abura age*
200 ml/7 fl oz *dashi* (page 153)
5 tablespoons sugar
6 tablespoons Japanese soy sauce
½ carrot
2 dried *shiitake*
20 g/¾ oz dried *kampyo*
salt
*Sushi Meshi* prepared from
275 g/10 oz Japanese rice (page 154)

AMERICAN
8 *abura age*
1 cup *dashi* (page 153)
5 tablespoons sugar
6 tablespoons Japanese soy sauce
½ carrot
2 dried *shiitake*
¾ oz dried *kampyo*
salt
*Sushi Meshi* prepared from 1⅓ cups
Japanese rice (page 154)

Put the *abura age* into a saucepan of boiling water. Bring back to the boil, then drain in a sieve and leave to cool. Cut the *abura age* in half widthways, then gently scoop away the inside to make a pocket.

Put the *dashi*, 4 tablespoons of the sugar and the *abura age* in a saucepan. Bring to the boil and boil gently for 5 to 6 minutes. Add 4 tablespoons of the soy sauce to the pan and continue to boil gently until most of the water has evaporated. Tilt the pan and baste the *abura age* while the sauce boils. Remove the pan from the heat and allow to cool.

Cut the carrot into very fine strips – *sengiri* style (see page 163). Put the carrot, 1½ teaspoons of the sugar and 3 tablespoons water in a saucepan. Bring to the boil, add 1 tablespoon of the soy sauce, then boil over a low to moderate heat until most of the water has evaporated, stirring well.

Soak the dried *shiitake* in warm water for 20 minutes, remove and discard the stems, then thinly slice the caps. Put the slices in a saucepan, then add the remaining sugar and 3 tablespoons water. Bring to the boil and add the last of the soy sauce. Boil over a low to moderate heat until most of the water has evaporated, stirring well.

Wash the *kampyo* in plenty of water. Pour off the water and squeeze the *kampyo* into a bowl. Sprinkle 2 tablespoons salt over the *kampyo* and crumple it with both hands for 5 minutes. Rinse and drain the *kampyo*, put it in a saucepan of boiling water and bring back to the boil. Boil gently for 4 to 5 minutes, then strain the *kampyo* in a sieve or colander. Leave to cool.

Make the *Sushi Meshi*, using 500 ml/17 fl oz [2 cups] water, following the recipe instructions. Mix all the prepared ingredients, except for the *kampyo*, with the warm rice. Stuff the rice mixture into the prepared *abura age* pockets. Fold up the edges of the *abura age* to enclose the filling, then tie each portion neatly with the *kampyo*. Arrange four portions of the food on each of four individual plates. **Serves 4**

# Sekihan

*—— Rice with Red Beans ——*

| METRIC/IMPERIAL | AMERICAN |
| --- | --- |
| 100 g/4 oz red beans | $\frac{2}{3}$ cup red beans |
| 350 g/12 oz Japanese rice | 2 cups Japanese rice |
| 75 g/3 oz glutinous rice | $\frac{1}{2}$ cup glutinous rice |
| 1 tablespoon black sesame seeds to garnish | 1 tablespoon black sesame seeds for garnish |
| salt to serve | salt for serving |

Soak the red beans in plenty of water for half a day. Drain and wash the beans in a bowl with cold running water. Put the beans with ten times their volume of water in a large saucepan. Bring to the boil, pour off the water, then pour in the same volume of fresh water. Bring back to the boil, then boil gently until the beans are tender, topping up with more boiling water as required. This should take about 1 hour.

Wash both types of rice, mixed, in a bowl with cold running water. Partly fill the bowl with water, stir the rice gently, pour off the water and repeat two or three more times. Drain the rice in a sieve or colander for about 30 to 60 minutes. This allows time for the rice to absorb some water and to partially soften the grains. Drain the beans through a sieve or colander. Put the beans, rice and 750 ml/1$\frac{1}{4}$ pints [3 cups] water in a heavy-based saucepan which has a tight-fitting lid.

Cover the pan, then bring to the boil over maximum heat and wait until the steam begins to appear around the edge of the lid. Lower the heat and simmer the rice gently for 12 to 13 minutes, keeping the lid tightly sealed all the time. Increase the heat to the maximum available and cook the rice for a further 10 seconds. (If you are cooking on an electric hob [stove], wait until the maximum temperature is reached before timing the 10 seconds.) Leave the saucepan with the lid on for about 10 to 15 minutes.

Remove the lid then fluff up the rice with a wooden spoon or serving spoon. Wrap the lid in a tea-towel [linen towel], replace it on the pan so that the towel lies between the lid and the saucepan until you are ready to serve the rice. Serve the rice hot in small individual bowls. Sprinkle a few black sesame seeds and salt on each portion. **Serves 4**

# Onigiri

—— *Rice Balls* ——

(Illustrated on pages 166/167)

| METRIC/IMPERIAL | AMERICAN |
| --- | --- |
| 425 g/15 oz Japanese rice | 2¼ cups Japanese rice |
| 5 g/¼ oz dried bonito fish | ¼ oz dried bonito fish |
| 1 tablespoon Japanese soy sauce | 1 tablespoon Japanese soy sauce |
| 2 *umeboshi* | 2 *umeboshi* |
| 50 g/2 oz sesame seeds, lightly roasted | ⅓ cup sesame seeds, lightly roasted |
| 1 sheet *nori* | 1 sheet *nori* |
| salt | salt |
| 12-cm/4½-in piece *takuan* to garnish | 4½-in piece *takuan* for garnish |

Wash the rice in a bowl with cold running water. Partly fill the bowl with water, stir the rice gently, pour off the water and repeat two or three more times. Drain the rice in a sieve or colander for about 30 to 60 minutes. This allows time for the rice to absorb some water and to partially soften the grains. Put the rice in a large heavy-based saucepan which has a tightly fitting lid. Pour in 750 ml/1¼ pints [3 cups] water.

Cover the pan, then bring to the boil over maximum heat and wait until the steam begins to appear around the edge of the lid. Lower the heat and simmer the rice gently for 12 to 13 minutes, keeping the lid tightly sealed all the time. Increase the heat to the maximum available and cook the rice for a further 10 seconds. (If you are cooking on an electric hob [stove], wait until the maximum temperature is reached before timing the 10 seconds.)

While the rice is cooking prepare the other ingredients. Mix the bonito fish with the soy sauce in a small bowl. Remove the stones [pits] from the *umeboshi*, then cut them in half. Put the sesame seeds on a plate.

Wave the *nori* sheet above a gas flame or electric ring for a few moments until it becomes light green. Take care not to burn yourself; if your hand feels too hot you are too close to the heat – about 13 cm/5 in away is normally correct. Cut the *nori* into eight pieces.

Prepare the garnish at this stage. Quarter the *takuan* lengthways and cut it into 5-mm/¼-in thick slices.

Pour 200 ml/7 fl oz [1 cup] water into a bowl and add a pinch of salt. When your hands become dry, dampen them with this water. Try to keep your hands just lightly moistened as you handle the rice. If they are too wet the rice will become too damp and the rice balls will not hold their shape correctly.

Put 3 tablespoons salt on a plate. Put 65–75 g/2½–3 oz [½ cup] hot rice into a small bowl (you should use hot rice because it shapes more easily and results in a better flavour) and make a hole in the centre. Put a little of the bonito fish mixture in the hole, then dust your damp hands with salt and pick up the rice. Squeeze the grains lightly to make a triangle shape enclosing the bonito fish mixture completely.

Repeat with the remaining rice making four *onigiri* filled with the fish, four with the *umeboshi* and four unfilled *onigiri*. Coat the plain *onigiri* with the sesame seeds. Wrap the fish and *umeboshi onigiri* in pieces of prepared *nori*.

Arrange one of each of the different *onigiri* on each of four small individual plates. Garnish each portion with the prepared *takuan*. Serve warm or cold; the *onigiri* are eaten with the fingers. **Serves 4**

# Green Pea Gohan

—— *Rice with Green Peas* ——

| METRIC/IMPERIAL | AMERICAN |
|---|---|
| 425 g/15 oz Japanese rice | 2¼ cups Japanese rice |
| 150 g/5 oz shelled peas | 1 cup shelled peas |
| 3 spring onions to garnish | 3 scallions to garnish |

Wash the rice in a bowl with cold running water. Partly fill the bowl with water, stir the rice gently, pour off the water and repeat two or three more times. Drain the rice in a sieve or colander for about 30 to 60 minutes.

Add the peas to boiling salted water, bring back to the boil, then boil for 1 minute. Drain the peas through a sieve or colander, reserving the cooking water. Pour this into a measuring jug and add enough water to give 750 ml/1¼ pints [3 cups]. Pour this into a heavy-based saucepan which has a lid, then add the peas and rice. Cover the pan and bring to the boil over maximum heat. Wait until steam begins to appear round the edge of the lid, then lower the heat and simmer gently for 12 to 13 minutes, keeping the lid tightly on the pan all the time. Increase the heat to the maximum available and cook the rice for a further 10 seconds, then remove the pan from the heat. Leave the saucepan with the lid on for about 10 to 15 minutes. Trim the spring onions [scallions] of roots and any bruised leaves then chop them finely. Remove the lid, add the chopped spring onions [scallions], then fluff up the rice. Wrap the lid in a clean tea-towel [linen towel] until you are ready to serve the rice. Serve the rice hot in small individual bowls. **Serves 4**

# Sunomono, Ae Mono

## — *Salads* —

These dishes consist of mixed ingredients with a rice vinegar sauce or a special dressing. They should have a fresh acid taste with a crunchy texture and they are intended to refresh the palate. You can use ingredients in many combinations but there are a few points to remember.

The preparation of the ingredients is very important; when you cook the ingredients before mixing them, you must allow them to cool down first then combine them. Drain any watery ingredients well before mixing them into the dish and mix the ingredients just before serving.

# Sunomono

*—— Vinegar Dressings for Japanese Salads ——*

### Sanbai Zu 1

| METRIC/IMPERIAL | AMERICAN |
| --- | --- |
| 100 ml/4 fl oz rice vinegar | $\frac{1}{2}$ cup rice vinegar |
| 1 tablespoon sugar | 1 tablespoon sugar |
| 1 tablespoon Japanese soy sauce | 1 tablespoon Japanese soy sauce |
| salt | salt |

Place all the ingredients in a bowl with 1 teaspoon salt and mix thoroughly.
Use as required.

### Sanbai Zu 2

| METRIC/IMPERIAL | AMERICAN |
| --- | --- |
| 100 ml/4 fl oz rice vinegar | $\frac{1}{2}$ cup rice vinegar |
| 150 ml/$\frac{1}{4}$ pint *dashi* (page 153) | $\frac{2}{3}$ cup *dashi* (page 153) |
| 1 tablespoon sugar | 1 tablespoon sugar |
| 1 tablespoon Japanese soy sauce | 1 tablespoon Japanese soy sauce |
| salt | salt |

Put all the ingredients in a small saucepan adding $\frac{1}{2}$ teaspoon salt and bring to
the boil over a low heat. When the sugar has dissolved, remove the pan from
the heat, then put the pan in a bowl of very cold water to cool the dressing
quickly.

### Nihai Zu

| METRIC/IMPERIAL | AMERICAN |
| --- | --- |
| 100 ml/4 fl oz rice vinegar | $\frac{1}{2}$ cup rice vinegar |
| 2 tablespoons Japanese soy sauce | 2 tablespoons Japanese soy sauce |
| 2 teaspoons *mirin* | 2 teaspoons *mirin* |

Put all the ingredients in a small bowl and mix thoroughly.

# Hana Renkon

—— *Lotus Root Flower Shapes* ——

(Illustrated on page 48)

| METRIC/IMPERIAL | AMERICAN |
|---|---|
| 100 g/4 oz fresh lotus root | $\frac{1}{4}$ lb fresh lotus root |
| 3 tablespoons rice vinegar | 3 tablespoons rice vinegar |
| 4 tablespoons *Sanbai Zu* (page 41) | $\frac{1}{4}$ cup *Sanbai Zu* (page 41) |
| 1 dried whole red chilli to garnish | 1 dried hot red pepper to garnish |

Peel the lotus root and cut away the sides to produce a flower shape. Slice the lotus root into 2-mm/$\frac{1}{10}$-in thick pieces. Mix 1 litre/1$\frac{3}{4}$ pints [1 quart[ water with the rice vinegar. Soak the lotus root slices in this mixture for 30 minutes, removing any scum which rises to the surface.

Drain the lotus root and put it in a saucepan with the *Sanbai Zu*. Add 4 tablespoons water, bring to the boil and boil over a low heat for about 10 minutes, stirring gently. Remove the pan from the heat and leave to cool.

Take off the chilli [hot pepper] stalk and remove the seeds gently from inside without splitting the shell. Slice thinly. Put the prepared lotus root into small individual bowls, then arrange the chilli [pepper] rings on top. **Serves 4**

# Horenso No Ohitashi

—— *Boiled Spinach* ——

(Illustrated on page 165)

| METRIC/IMPERIAL | AMERICAN |
|---|---|
| 400 g/14 oz fresh spinach | 1 lb fresh bulk spinach |
| salt | salt |
| 7 g/$\frac{1}{4}$ oz dried bonito fish | $\frac{1}{4}$ oz dried bonito fish |
| 1 tablespoon sesame seeds, lightly roasted, to garnish | 1 tablespoon sesame seeds, lightly roasted, for garnish |
| 4 tablespoons Japanese soy sauce | $\frac{1}{4}$ cup Japanese soy sauce |

Wash the spinach leaves one by one under running water, removing any tough veins and bruised leaves. Lay the leaves with the stems together and make them into neat bundles. Put the spinach bundles into a saucepan of boiling salted water so that only the stems are immersed initially. Bring back to the boil, then push all the spinach down into the water. Boil for 1 to 1$\frac{1}{2}$ minutes.

Remove the spinach bundles and put the leaves into cold water to cool. Hold the stems together as before and squeeze the water out of the leaves with one hand. Cut the leaves to equal length, then across into 3.5-cm/1½-in wide pieces. Arrange the spinach on four small individual plates, spreading it out lightly. Sprinkle the bonito fish over and between the spinach. Sprinkle the sesame seeds on top and pour 1 tablespoon soy sauce over each portion just before serving. **Serves 4**

# Moyashi No Wasabi Ae

—— *Bean Sprouts with Japanese Green Mustard* ——

(Illustrated on pages 86/87)

| METRIC/IMPERIAL | AMERICAN |
|---|---|
| 225 g/8 oz fresh bean sprouts | ½ lb fresh bean sprouts (about 4 cups) |
| salt | salt |
| ⅓ cucumber | ⅓ cucumber |
| *Dressing* | *Dressing* |
| 4 tablespoons rice vinegar | ¼ cup rice vinegar |
| 1 tablespoon sugar | 1 tablespoon sugar |
| 1 tablespoon Japanese soy sauce | 1 tablespoon Japanese soy sauce |
| ½ teaspoon *wasabi* | ½ teaspoon *wasabi* |

Wash the bean sprouts thoroughly in a few changes of clean water. Remove the husks from the seeds as you wash the sprouts. Put the bean sprouts into boiling salted water and bring to the boil. Boil for 30 seconds, then drain and soak in cold water to cool. Drain the bean sprouts, tossing them in a sieve to remove the last of the water.

Sprinkle 1 tablespoon salt over the cucumber, then rub it against a chopping board for ½ to 1 minute. Put the cucumber into boiling water for a few moments, then drain and soak it in cold water. This method ensures that the cucumber will have a clear colour. Cut the cucumber in half lengthways, then slice it thinly crossways.

Mix the ingredients for the dressing, adding ½ teaspoon salt. Gently toss the prepared bean sprouts and cucumber together, then pour in the dressing and mix well. Arrange small heaps of the salad in small individual bowls. **Serves 4**

# Kawari Oroshi Ae

—— *White Radish Salad* ——

(Illustrated opposite)

| METRIC/IMPERIAL | AMERICAN |
|---|---|
| 225 g/8 oz large white radish | ½ lb large white radish |
| 1 dried *kikurage* | 1 dried *kikurage* |
| 1 teaspoon Japanese soy sauce | 1 teaspoon Japanese soy sauce |
| 1 teaspoon *sake* | 1 teaspoon *sake* |
| 2 eggs | 2 eggs |
| 10 *mitsuba* or 6-cm/2½-in piece cucumber | 10 *mitsuba* or 2½-in piece cucumber |
| *benishoga* (red ginger pickles) | *benishoga* (red ginger pickles) |
| 3 tablespoons *San Bai Zu* (page 41) | 3 tablespoons *San Bai Zu* (page 41) |

Peel and grate the radish, then put it on a *makisu* (bamboo blind) or in a sieve and allow it to drain naturally; do not squeeze the radish. Soak the *kikurage* in warm water for 20 minutes, then cut it thinly lengthways.

Put the soy sauce and *sake* in a small saucepan. Add the *kikurage* and cook over a low to moderate heat, until most of the water has evaporated. Remove the pan from the heat and allow to cool.

Prepare the eggs following the technique for *Usu Yaki Tamago* (see page 155). Cut the cooked eggs into pieces measuring $3 \times 0.5$ cm/$1\frac{1}{4} \times \frac{1}{2}$ in. Remove and wash the roots and leaves from the *mitsuba*. Put the stems in boiling salted water, bring back to the boil and boil for 30 seconds. Drain and soak in cold water, then drain and cut them into 3-cm/$1\frac{1}{4}$-in long pieces. If you use cucumber, cut it in half crossways, then cut it following the *sen roppon* technique (see page 163). Soak in water for a few moments and drain the cucumber, tossing it in a sieve to remove the last of the water.

Cut the *benishoga* for the garnish in a *matsuba giri* style (see page 169) to make 4 pieces. Mix the prepared ingredients (apart from the garnish) with the *Sanbai Zu* and arrange the salad in small heaps in small individual bowls. Put the prepared garnish on top. **Serves 4**

**Opposite page** *Top: Kawari Oroshi Ae; bottom: Onigiri (page 38)*
**Overleaf** *Clockwise from the top: Tori Wasa (page 50), Kani No Shoga Zu (page 51) and Kyuri To Wakame No Sunomono (page 50)*

# Tako Su

—— *Octopus with Vinegar Dressing* ——

(Illustrated opposite)

| METRIC/IMPERIAL | AMERICAN |
|---|---|
| 225 g/8 oz octopus legs | $\frac{1}{2}$ lb octopus legs |
| $4\frac{1}{2}$ teaspoons rice vinegar | $4\frac{1}{2}$ teaspoons rice vinegar |
| $\frac{1}{2}$ cucumber | $\frac{1}{2}$ cucumber |
| salt | salt |
| 15 g/$\frac{1}{4}$ oz fresh root ginger | $\frac{1}{4}$ oz fresh ginger root |
| 100 ml/4 fl oz *Nihai Zu* (page 41) | $\frac{1}{2}$ cup *Nihai Zu* (page 41) |
| *Shoga Amazu Zuke* (page 138) to garnish | *Shoga Amazu Zuke* (page 138) for garnish |

Add the octopus legs to a saucepan of boiling water, bring back to the boil, then boil for 5 to 6 minutes or until the octopus floats to the top of the water. Drain the octopus in a sieve or colander and cut the legs crossways into 1.5-cm/$\frac{3}{4}$-in wide pieces. Put these pieces into a bowl and pour in the rice vinegar. Stir well, then leave to marinate for 5 minutes. Drain the octopus and toss the pieces in a sieve or colander to remove the last of the vinegar.

Cut the cucumber in half lengthways and slice it thinly crossways. Soak the slices in salted water for 10 minutes, then drain and squeeze them lightly. Peel and grate the fresh root ginger, then mix it with the octopus and cucumber. Add the *Nihai Zu* and toss all the ingredients together gently.

Slice the ginger pickles thinly with the grain, then cut each slice thinly into strips, again cutting with the grain (*sengiri* style, see page 163).

Arrange small heaps of the salad in small individual bowls, with all the ingredients showing distinctly. Put some of the red ginger pickles on top and serve. **Serves 4**

*Top: Tako Su; bottom: Hana Renkon (page 42)*

# Kyuri To Wakame No Sunomono

*—— Cucumber and Seaweed with Vinegar Dressing ——*

(Illustrated on pages 46/47)

| METRIC/IMPERIAL | AMERICAN |
|---|---|
| $\frac{1}{2}$ cucumber | $\frac{1}{2}$ cucumber |
| 15 g/$\frac{1}{4}$ oz dried *wakame* | $\frac{1}{4}$ oz dried *wakame* |
| 100 ml/4 fl oz *Sanbai Zu* (page 41) | $\frac{1}{2}$ cup *Sanbai Zu* (page 41) |
| juice of $\frac{1}{2}$ lemon | juice of $\frac{1}{2}$ lemon |
| *Shoga Amazu Zuke* (page 138) to garnish | *Shoga Amazu Zuke* (page 138) for garnish |

Cut the cucumber in half lengthways, then slice it thinly crossways. Soak the slices in salted water for 10 minutes, then drain and lightly squeeze them. Soak the *wakame* in water for 5 to 10 minutes, then when it has fully expanded, cut it crossways into 3-cm/1$\frac{1}{4}$-in wide pieces. Put the *wakame* into boiling water, then drain it, tossing the pieces in a sieve to remove the last of the water.

Blend the *Sanbai Zu* and the lemon juice in a bowl, then mix in all the other ingredients. Cut the red ginger pickles into four pieces in a *matsuba giri* style (see page 169). Arrange small neat heaps of the salad in small individual bowls and put the red ginger pickles on top. **Serves 4**

# Tori Wasa

*—— Chicken and Cucumber Salad ——*

(Illustrated on pages 46/47)

| METRIC/IMPERIAL | AMERICAN |
|---|---|
| 400 g/14 oz chicken breasts | 1 large chicken breast (about 14 oz) |
| $\frac{1}{2}$ cucumber | $\frac{1}{2}$ cucumber |
| 8-cm/3$\frac{1}{4}$-in piece large white radish | 3$\frac{1}{4}$-in piece large white radish |
| *Dressing* | *Dressing* |
| 4 tablespoons Japanese soy sauce | 4 tablespoons Japanese soy sauce |
| 1 teaspoon *wasabi* | 1 teaspoon *wasabi* |

Remove the skin, bone and any gristle from the chicken. Put the meat into a saucepan of boiling water. Bring back to the boil, then boil for 5 to 6 minutes or until the chicken is just cooked through; do not overcook. Drain the chicken in a sieve or colander, then leave to cool. Cut the meat against the grain into 5-mm/$\frac{1}{4}$-in wide pieces.

Cut the cucumber crossways into 4-cm/1$\frac{1}{2}$-in long pieces, then cut these in a *sen roppon* style (see page 163). Similarly, cut the large white radish in a *sen roppon* style. Soak the cucumber and the radish in water for 1 to 2 minutes. Drain them and toss the pieces in a sieve to remove the last of the water.

Mix the ingredients together, tossing them gently, and arrange neat heaps of the salad in small individual bowls. Mix the dressing ingredients and pour on top just before serving. **Serves 4**

# Kani No Shoga Zu

—— *Crab with Vinegar Dressing* ——

(Illustrated on pages 46/47)

| METRIC/IMPERIAL | AMERICAN |
|:---:|:---:|
| 1 (169-g/6-oz) can crab meat, drained | 1 (8-oz) can crabmeat, drained |
| 2 eggs | 2 eggs |
| $\frac{1}{2}$ cucumber | $\frac{1}{2}$ cucumber |
| 2 dried *kikurage* | 2 dried *kikurage* |
| 15 g/$\frac{1}{4}$ oz fresh root ginger | $\frac{1}{4}$ oz fresh ginger root |
| 100 ml/4 fl oz *Sanbai Zu* (page 41) | $\frac{1}{2}$ cup *Sanbai Zu* (page 41) |
| *Shoga Amazu Zuke* (page 138) to garnish | *Shoga Amazu Zuke* (page 138) for garnish |

Divide the crab into medium-sized pieces; do not make the pieces too small. Prepare the eggs following the *usuyaki tamago* technique (see page 155), then cut the cooked eggs into oblong pieces measuring 2.5 × 0.5 cm/1 × $\frac{1}{4}$ in.

Cut the cucumber in half lengthways, then slice it thinly crossways. Soak the cucumber slices in salted water for 10 minutes, then drain and lightly squeeze them. Soak the *kikurage* in warm water for 20 minutes, then cut it up thinly lengthways. Peel and grate the fresh root ginger.

Blend the *Sanbai Zu* with the prepared ginger. Mix all the prepared ingredients with the *Sanbai Zu* and ginger, tossing them all gently. Slice the *Shoga Amazu Zuke* thinly with the grain, then cut it again into thin pieces with the grain (*sengiri* style, see page 163).

Arrange small heaps of the salad in small individual bowls so that each of the ingredients are shown distinctly. Put some of the prepared garnish on top. **Serves 4**

# Nabe Mono

## —— *Cooking at the Table* ——

All the dishes in this chapter are cooked at the table. Serve rice and *sake* with this type of meal as they are good accompaniments. This type of meal is excellent to serve at a dinner party, especially in winter. There is a wide selection of ingredients to choose from but note the following points. You should choose fresh ingredients, particularly seafood and meat; vegetables are less important. While the meal is eaten, keep the flavour of the stock fixed. Make sure the amount of stock is adequate and keep it simmering.

In addition to the recipes, you can serve extra ingredients with the meal. For example, try chopped spring onions [scallions], peeled and grated white radish, chilli powder or peeled and grated fresh root ginger.

## Yose Nabe

### —— *Fish Nabe* ——

| METRIC/IMPERIAL | AMERICAN |
|---|---|
| 225 g/8 oz small haddock fillets | $\frac{1}{2}$ lb small haddock fillets |
| 225 g/8 oz squid (the bigger and heavier the better) | $\frac{1}{2}$ lb squid (the bigger and heavier the better) |
| 8 uncooked whole Mediterranean prawns | 8 raw Jumbo shrimp |
| 2 chicken leg joints | 2 chicken legs-with-thighs |
| 225 g/8 oz fresh spinach | $\frac{1}{2}$ lb fresh spinach |
| bunch of spring onions (those with thick stems are better) or leeks | bunch of scallions (those with thick stems are better) or leeks |
| 8 button mushrooms | 8 button mushrooms |
| *Stock* | *Stock* |
| 1.15 litres/2 pints *dashi* (page 153) | 5 cups *dashi* (page 153) |
| 1$\frac{1}{2}$ teaspoon salt | 1$\frac{1}{2}$ teaspoon salt |
| 4 tablespoons *sake* | $\frac{1}{4}$ cup *sake* |
| 4 tablespoons *mirin* | $\frac{1}{4}$ cup *mirin* |
| 4 tablespoons Japanese soy sauce | $\frac{1}{4}$ cup Japanese soy sauce |

Skin the haddock fillets, then cut them crossways into 3.5-cm/$1\frac{1}{2}$-in wide pieces. Prepare the squid following method 1 on page 160. Using a sharp, straight-edged knife, score the squid diagonally at 2-mm/$\frac{1}{10}$-in intervals, then again at right angles to make diamond marks on the squid skin. Cut the squid into 3.5-cm/$1\frac{1}{2}$-in squares and put the pieces into a saucepan of boiling water. Bring back to the boil, then immediately drain the pieces in a sieve.

Shell the prawns [shrimp] leaving their tails on, then use a cocktail stick to take out the veins. Prepare the chicken following the instructions on page 159, cutting the meat crossways into 3-cm/$1\frac{1}{4}$-in wide pieces. Wash the spinach leaves one by one under running water, removing any tough veins and bruised leaves. Put the stems together and make the leaves into neat bundles. Remove the roots and any bruised leaves from the spring onions [scallions] or leeks, then wash and cut the rest at a slant into pieces measuring 3.5 cm/$1\frac{1}{2}$ in long. Wash the mushrooms. Arrange all the prepared ingredients on a big serving plate, keeping them separate.

Mix all the ingredients for the stock in a bowl, then pour 600–900 ml/$1-1\frac{1}{2}$ pints [$2\frac{1}{2}$–3 cups] of it into a *donabe* (a shallow Japanese pan) or a shallow saucepan. Bring to the boil, then put the pan on a spirit burner or an electric heater for serving at the table. Set the heater so that the stock is just simmering.

Put some of each of the seafood and chicken in the pan. Bring back to the boil and simmer for 2 to 3 minutes, removing any scum which rises to the surface. Then add the vegetables, keeping the ingredients separate. Simmer until the seafood is cooked and the vegetables are tender. You may have to add further stock as the liquid evaporates during the meal. Set out a small bowl and chopsticks for each person, so that they can take a little of the hot food as it is cooked. **Serves 4**

# Tori No Mizutaki

—— *Chicken Nabe* ——

| METRIC/IMPERIAL | AMERICAN |
|---|---|
| 4 chicken leg joints | 4 chicken legs-with-thighs |
| 8 mushrooms | 8 mushrooms |
| 8 Chinese leaves | 8 leaves *bok choy* |
| salt | salt |
| 225 g/8 oz fresh spinach | $\frac{1}{2}$ lb fresh bulk spinach |
| 2 bunches spring onions (those with thick stems are better) | 2 bunches scallions (those with thick stems are better) |
| 225 g/8 oz *tofu* | $\frac{1}{2}$ lb *tofu* |
| *Dipping Sauce* | *Dipping Sauce* |
| (Allow extra ingredients to top up the sauce during the meal) | (Allow extra ingredients to top up the sauce during the meal) |
| 8 tablespoons Japanese soy sauce | $\frac{1}{2}$ cup Japanese soy sauce |
| 2 tablespoons lemon juice | 2 tablespoons lemon juice |

Prepare the chicken following the instructions on page 159. Remove and discard the skin from the chicken. Cut the meat crossways into 3.5-cm/$1\frac{1}{2}$-in wide pieces.

Wash the mushrooms, and make V-shaped cuts from the centre outwards around the top. Remove a piece of mushroom from alternate cuts. Put the Chinese leaves [*bok choy*] in boiling salted water, bring back to the boil, then boil for 1 minute. Drain the leaves, then remove them from the water and unfold each on to a chopping board or a baking tray. Sprinkle 1 teaspoon salt over the leaves.

Wash the spinach leaves one by one under running water, removing any tough veins and bruised leaves. Lay the stems together and make the leaves into bundles. Put the spinach bundles into boiling salted water so that only the stems are immersed initially. Bring back to the boil, then push all the spinach down into the water. Boil for 1 to $1\frac{1}{2}$ minutes. Remove the spinach and put the leaves into cold water to cool. Drain, hold the stems together as before and squeeze the water out of the leaves with one hand.

Lay out a *makisu* (bamboo blind) with the strands of wood running from left to right. Put four of the Chinese leaves [*bok choy*] on the blind so that they overlap each other with the root ends lying alternately towards the left and right edges of the blind. Repeat using half the spinach shoots so that they are aligned on top of the Chinese leaves [*bok choy*]. Using the bamboo blind as a guide, roll up the Chinese leaves [*bok choy*] tightly. Repeat once more for the remaining Chinese leaves [*bok choy*] and spinach. Cut the rolled vegetables across into 3.5-cm/$1\frac{1}{2}$-in wide slices. You can use just Chinese leaves [*bok choy*] without any spinach if you like.

Remove and discard the spring onion [scallion] roots and any bruised leaves, then wash and cut three-quarters of the onions at a slant into 3.5-cm/1½-in long pieces. Alternatively you can use leeks instead of the spring onions [scallions]. Chop the remaining spring onions [scallions] finely, then set them aside for use in the dipping sauce. Cut the *tofu* into eight pieces. Arrange all the prepared ingredients, except the chicken, on a big serving plate, keeping them separate.

Pour 600–900 ml/1–1½ pints [2½–3 cups] water into a *donabe* (a shallow Japanese pan) or a shallow saucepan and bring to the boil. Put the chicken in and bring back to the boil again, then simmer until the meat is just cooked, removing any scum which rises to the surface.

Move the pan on to a spirit burner or an electric heater suitable for serving at the table. Put some of each of the ingredients in the pan, keeping them separate and cook until the food is tender. Always keep the water just simmering. As the liquid evaporates replenish it with a little fresh water.

Prepare four small individual soup bowls: place 2 tablespoons of the Japanese soy sauce and some of the chopped spring onions [scallions] into each, then add 1½ teaspoons of the lemon juice to each. You can add fresh soy sauce, spring onions [scallions] and lemon juice when the sauce becomes too watery. If you wish, you can serve *Ponzu Joyu* (see page 156) as an additional dipping sauce.

At the table each person selects and cooks pieces of the prepared food. Using chopsticks, the hot food is dipped into individual bowls of sauce and eaten. **Serves 4**

# Shabu Shabu

—— *Simmered Beef with Vegetables* ——

(Illustrated on page 65)

| METRIC/IMPERIAL | AMERICAN |
|---|---|
| 450–575 g/1–1¾ lb good quality beef or silverside | 1–1¾ lb good quality beef such as flank steak |
| 8 button mushrooms | 8 button mushrooms |
| 225-g/8-oz *tofu* | ½ lb *tofu* |
| 8 Chinese leaves | 8 leaves *bok choy* |
| salt | salt |
| 225 g/8 oz fresh spinach | ½ lb fresh bulk spinach |
| 225 g/8 oz fresh bean sprouts | ½ lb fresh bean sprouts (about 4 cups) |
| 2 bunches spring onions | |
| 10-cm/4-in square *kombu* | 2 bunches scallions |
| 1 carrot to garnish | 4-in square *kombu* |
| *Dipping Sauce* | 1 carrot for garnish |
| (Allow extra ingredients to top up the sauce during the meal) | *Dipping Sauce* |
| | (Allow extra ingredients to replenish the sauce during the meal) |
| 8 tablespoons Japanese soy sauce | ½ cup Japanese soy sauce |
| 2 tablespoons lemon juice | 2 tablespoons lemon juice |

Peel the carrot and score away the sides to produce a flower shape, then slice it for the garnish. Set aside.

Trim any fat from the meat and slice the meat very thinly against the grain. Half-frozen meat is easy to slice thinly, so if you have time put the piece of beef in the freezer for a while first. Wash the mushrooms. Make V-shaped cuts from the centre outwards around the top. Remove a piece of mushroom from alternate cuts. Cut the *tofu* into eight pieces.

Put the Chinese leaves [*bok choy*] in boiling salted water, bring back to the boil, then boil for 1 minute. Drain the leaves, remove them from the water and unfold them on to a chopping board or a baking tray. Sprinkle 1 teaspoon salt over the leaves.

Wash the spinach leaves one by one under running water, removing any tough veins and bruised leaves. Place the stems together and make the leaves into bundles. Hold the bundles together. Put the spinach bundles into boiling salted water so that only the stems are immersed initially. Bring back to the boil and push all the spinach down into the water, then boil for 1 to 1½ minutes. Remove the spinach – the leaves will be separate. Put these into cold water to cool. Put the stems together as before and squeeze the water out of the leaves with one hand.

Lay out a *makisu* (bamboo blind), with the strands of wood running from left to right. Put four of the Chinese leaves [*bok choy*] on the blind so that they overlap each other with the root ends alternately towards the left and right edges of the blind. Lay half the spinach leaves on top so that they are aligned with the Chinese leaves [*bok choy*]. Using the bamboo blind as a guide, roll up the Chinese leaves [*bok choy*] tightly. Repeat once more for the remaining Chinese leaves [*bok choy*] and spinach. Cut the rolled vegetables across into 3.5-cm/1½-in thick slices.

If you like you can use just Chinese leaves [*bok choy*] without the spinach. Put the bean sprouts in a sieve and wash them under running water, toss them in the sieve to remove the last of the water. Remove the spring onion [scallion] roots and any bruised leaves, then wash and drain them. Cut three-quarters of the spring onions [*scallions*] into 3.5-cm/1½-in long pieces; cut the pieces at an angle so that the cut edges slant. Finely chop the reserved spring onions [*scallions*] then put them in a small bowl and set aside to use in the dipping sauce.

Wipe the *kombu* with absorbent kitchen paper and make three or four crossways cuts three-quarters of the way through. Put the *kombu* in a saucepan and pour in 1.15 litres/2 pints [5 cups] water. Bring to the boil over a low to moderate heat, then strain the liquid immediately, discarding the kelp but keeping the stock.

Arrange all the prepared ingredients attractively on a big serving plate and garnish with the flower-shaped carrot slices.

Pour 600–900 ml/1–1½ pints [2½–3 cups] of the *kombu* stock into a *donabe* (a shallow Japanese pan) or a shallow saucepan. Bring to the boil, then put the pan on a spirit burner or an electric heater for serving at the table. Keep the stock simmering. You can add more of the remaining stock as it evaporates. Put some of each of the ingredients in the pan and cook for 1 to 2 minutes until the meat is just cooked and the vegetables are tender. Remove any scum as it rises to the surface of the stock.

Prepare four small individual soup bowls: place 2 tablespoons of the Japanese soy sauce, some of the chopped spring onions [scallions] and 1½ teaspoons of the lemon juice in each. You may have to add more soy sauce, onions and lemon juice when the sauce becomes too watery. If you wish, you can serve *Ponzu Joyu* (page 156) as an additional sauce for dipping the food.

To eat, dip the cooked ingredients from the pan into the sauce with chopsticks. Each person takes some of the freshly cooked ingredients from the pan and dips them in the sauce. More ingredients are added to the pan and cooked during the meal. The stock should be topped up as it evaporates.
**Serves 4**

# Sukiyaki

—— *Simmered Beef* ——

(Illustrated on page 165)

| METRIC/IMPERIAL | AMERICAN |
|---|---|
| 450 g/1 lb good-quality beef (fillet or silverside) | 1 lb good-quality beef such as flank steak |
| bunch of spring onions | bunch of scallions |
| 2 medium onions | 2 medium-size onions |
| 1 (250-g/9-oz) can *shirataki*, drained | 1 (9-oz) can *shirataki*, drained |
| 4 Chinese leaves | 4 leaves *bok choy* |
| 225 g/8 oz *tofu* | $\frac{1}{2}$ lb *tofu* |
| *Sauce* | *Sauce* |
| 50 ml/2 fl oz Japanese soy sauce | $\frac{1}{4}$ cup Japanese soy sauce |
| 50 ml/2 fl oz *sake* | $\frac{1}{4}$ cup *sake* |
| 3 tablespoons sugar | 3 tablespoons sugar |
| $\frac{1}{2}$ teaspoon chilli powder (optional) | $\frac{1}{2}$ teaspoon chilli powder (optional) |
| 2 tablespoons oil for cooking | 2 tablespoons oil for cooking |

Trim off and discard any fat from the meat then place it in the freezer until half frozen. Slice the meat very thinly against the grain into pieces about 5-cm/2-in square. Remove the spring onion [scallion] roots and any bruised leaves, then wash and cut the remainder crossways into pieces measuring 3.5-cm/1$\frac{1}{2}$-in long. Peel and cut the onions in half vertically, then cut them crossways into 5-mm/$\frac{1}{4}$-in thick slices. Put the *shirataki* into a saucepan of boiling water, bring back to the boil, then immediately drain in a sieve. Cut the *shirataki* into pieces about 5-cm/2-in long. Cut the Chinese leaves [*bok choy*] crossways into 3.5-cm/1$\frac{1}{2}$-in wide pieces. Cut the *tofu* into eight pieces. Mix the sauce ingredients in a small bowl, adding the chilli powder to taste when the other ingredients are mixed.

Thoroughly heat a shallow saucepan or frying pan. Pour in the oil, then add the meat, stirring well. When the meat is almost cooked pour the sauce into the pan. Bring to the boil, then collect the meat at one side of the pan. Bring to the boil, then collect the meat at one side of the pan. Put all the remaining ingredients in the pan, keeping each type separate. If the pan is not large enough to hold all the ingredients at once, cook the ingredients in batches. Bring to the boil again and put a lid on the pan, then reduce to a low or moderate heat and simmer for 6 to 7 minutes. Put the pan on an electric table heater or spirit burner for serving at the table. Using chopsticks, each person should take a little of the hot food. **Serves 4**

# Yakiniku

—— *Korean-style Barbecue* ——

(Illustrated on pages 166/167)

| METRIC/IMPERIAL | AMERICAN |
|---|---|
| 450 g/1 lb good-quality beef (silverside or topside) | 1 lb good-quality beef such as flank steak |
| 1 green pepper | 1 green pepper |
| 1 aubergine or 8 button mushrooms | 1 eggplant or 8 button mushrooms |
| *Tare* | *Tare* |
| 3–5 cloves garlic | 3–5 cloves garlic |
| 3 spring onions | 3 scallions |
| 100 ml/4 fl oz Japanese soy sauce | $\frac{1}{2}$ cup Japanese soy sauce |
| 1–1$\frac{1}{2}$ teaspoons chilli powder | 1–1$\frac{1}{2}$ teaspoons chilli powder |
| freshly ground black pepper | freshly ground black pepper |
| oil for cooking | oil for cooking |

Trim off and discard any fat from the meat and place it in the freezer until it is half frozen. Slice the meat very thinly to make 5-cm/2-in squares.

Cut the green pepper in half vertically then remove the stalk, pith and seeds. Cut each half into four quarters. Remove the stalk off the aubergine [eggplant] and wash the vegetable. Cut it in half lengthways, then slice it crossways into pieces which are 5 mm/$\frac{1}{4}$ in thick. If you leave the aubergine [eggplant] for a long time after cutting, the pieces will become dark in colour, so cut it just before preparing the *tare*. If you use the mushrooms, wash them and cut them in half.

To make the *tare* peel and crush the garlic, remove the spring onion [scallion] roots and any bruised leaves, then wash and finely chop the remainder. Mix all *tare* ingredients thoroughly in a bowl.

Put the meat in the *tare*, stir gently, and allow it to marinate for 20 to 30 minutes. Remove the meat from the *tare* mixture and put it on a big serving plate. Put the aubergine [eggplant] in the bowl, mix it with the remaining *tare* but it is not necessary to completely submerge the vegetables in the mixture. Put the green pepper and the aubergine [eggplant] on the serving plate, keeping each ingredient separate.

Put a shallow saucepan or frying pan on an electric table heater or good spirit burner for serving at the table. Allow the pan to become hot, then pour in 2 tablespoons oil. Put some of the meat and vegetables into the pan, allow the pan to cool slightly to a moderate heat, then fry for 2 to 4 minutes or until the meat is cooked and the vegetables are tender. Add more oil and continue cooking the ingredients in this way.

Each person should take some of the freshly cooked ingredients. More food is added to the pan as necessary during the meal. **Serves 4**

# Teppan Yaki

—— *Beef and Vegetable Barbecue* ——

| METRIC/IMPERIAL | AMERICAN |
|---|---|
| 450 g/1 lb good-quality beef (topside or silverside) | 1 lb good-quality beef such as flank steak |
| freshly ground black pepper | freshly ground black pepper |
| 1 aubergine | 1 eggplant |
| salt | salt |
| 2 medium onions | 2 medium-size onions |
| 1 medium carrot | 1 medium-size carrot |
| 225 g/8 oz bean sprouts | $\frac{1}{2}$ lb fresh bean sprouts (about 4 cups) |
| 8 button mushrooms | 8 button mushrooms |
| *Dipping Sauce* | *Dipping Sauce* |
| (Allow extra ingredients to top up the sauce during the meal) | (Allow extra ingredients to replenish the sauce during the meal) |
| 8 tablespoons Japanese soy sauce | $\frac{1}{2}$ cup Japanese soy sauce |
| 8 tablespoons lemon juice | $\frac{1}{2}$ cup lemon juice |
| oil for cooking | oil for cooking |

Trim off and discard any fat from the meat then place it in a freezer until half frozen. Cut the meat against the grain into pieces measuring about 5 cm/2 in square. Sprinkle pepper on both sides of each slice.

Remove and discard the stalk off the aubergine [eggplant] and wash the vegetable. Slice the aubergine [eggplant] across into 5-mm/$\frac{1}{4}$-in thick pieces, then soak these in salted water for 5 to 10 minutes, removing any scum which rises to the surface. Drain the aubergine [eggplant] in a sieve or colander, then lay the pieces on absorbent kitchen paper to drain thoroughly. Peel and slice the onions into 5-mm/$\frac{1}{4}$-in pieces. Peel and slice the carrot at an angle into 5-mm/$\frac{1}{4}$-in thick pieces. Wash the bean sprouts in a few changes of clean water. Remove the husks of the beans and drain the sprouts thoroughly in a sieve. Wash the mushrooms and cut them in half. Arrange all the prepared ingredients attractively on a big serving plate, keeping them separate.

For dipping, pour 2 tablespoons of the soy sauce and 1$\frac{1}{2}$ teaspoons of the lemon juice into each of four individual small bowls. Serve this dipping sauce at the table, adding further soy sauce and lemon juice as necessary.

Put a frying pan on an electric table heater or spirit burner for serving at the table. Allow the pan to become hot, then pour in 2 tablespoons oil. Put some of the meat and vegetables into the pan, allow the pan to cool slightly to a moderate heat, then fry the ingredients for 2 to 4 minutes or until the meat is cooked and the vegetables are tender. Continue cooking the ingredients in this way. Using chopsticks, each person should take a little of the hot, freshly cooked food and dip it in the prepared sauce. **Serves 4**

# Butaniku No Misodare Yaki

—— *Pork Barbecue* ——

| METRIC/IMPERIAL | AMERICAN |
|---|---|
| 450 g/1 lb boneless loin of pork | 1 lb boneless loin of pork |
| 8 button mushrooms | 8 button mushrooms |
| bunch of spring onions | bunch of scallions |
| *Tare* | *Tare* |
| 2 cloves garlic | 2 cloves garlic |
| 5 g/¼ oz fresh root ginger | ¼ oz fresh ginger root |
| 2 tablespoons red *miso* | 2 tablespoons red *miso* |
| 100 ml/4 fl oz Japanese soy sauce | ½ cup Japanese soy sauce |
| 2 tablespoons *sake* | 2 tablespoons *sake* |
| freshly ground black pepper | freshly ground black pepper |
| oil for cooking | oil for cooking |

Trim off and discard any fat from the meat. Place it in the freezer until half frozen, then slice it thinly against the grain into 5-cm/2-in squares. Wash the mushrooms. Remove the spring onion [scallion] roots and any bruised leaves, then wash the rest. Cut the onions across in half and keep the top part for the *tare*. Cut the lower parts of the spring onions [scallions] into 3.5-cm/1½-in long pieces.

To make the *tare* peel and crush the garlic; peel and grate the ginger. Finely chop the reserved top parts of the spring onions [scallions]. Put the *miso* into a big mixing bowl and add the soy sauce, stirring to make a smooth mixture. Add all the remaining *tare* ingredients to the bowl and mix thoroughly.

Put the meat in the bowl with the *tare* and stir lightly, then leave to marinate for 20 to 30 minutes. Remove the meat from the *tare* (marinade) and arrange it on a big serving plate, then put the mushrooms in the bowl and mix them with the remaining marinade.

Put a shallow saucepan or frying pan on an electric table heater or spirit burner for serving at the table. Allow the pan to become hot, then pour in 2 tablespoons of the oil. Put some of the meat and vegetables into the pan, allow the pan to cool slightly to a moderate heat, then fry the ingredients for 2 to 4 minutes or until the meat is cooked and the vegetables are tender.

Using chopsticks, people help themselves to the ingredients from the pan. More oil is added to the pan and the ingredients are cooked as necessary.
**Serves 4**

# Age Mono

## *—— Deep Fried Dishes ——*

This method of cooking is used for frying plain or battered ingredients in hot vegetable oil. There are several variations: *Su Age*, *Kara Age*, *Koromo Age* and *Kawari Age*. They are all very simple but you need to care for your utensils, ingredients and the order in which you cook the food. The following notes will help you to achieve good results.

1 Fried food should be light and crisp. You should keep the oil temperature fixed and avoid putting too many ingredients in the oil at once. Use a thick saucepan of moderate depth and size so as to maintain the oil temperature.

2 It is better to use fresh oil, especially for *tempura*. If you use the same oil many times, the oil will become oxidised, indigestible and unsuitable for light frying.

3 You should always use fresh ingredients. If you do not use fresh seafood for *tempura* the ingredients will contain too much water and will then slip out of the batter after cooking. The colour of the food will also be inferior.

## Karei Kara Age

### *—— Fried Flounder ——*

| METRIC/IMPERIAL | AMERICAN |
|---|---|
| 2 flounders | 2 flounders |
| pepper | pepper |
| *Dipping Sauce* | *Dipping Sauce* |
| 200 ml/7 fl oz *dashi* (page 153) | 1 cup *dashi* (page 153) |
| 3 tablespoons *mirin* | 3 tablespoons *mirin* |
| 3 tablespoons Japanese soy sauce | 3 tablespoons Japanese soy sauce |
| 5 g/$\frac{1}{4}$ oz dried bonito fish | $\frac{1}{4}$ oz dried bonito fish |
| 10-cm/4-in piece large white radish | 4-in piece large white radish |
| oil for deep frying | oil for deep frying |
| *Garnish* | *Garnish* |
| 8 fresh green asparagus spears | 8 fresh green asparagus spears |
| 1 lemon, cut into 8 wedges | 1 lemon, cut into 8 wedges |
| plain flour for coating | flour for coating |

First make the dipping sauce: put all the ingredients except the bonito fish and white radish into a saucepan. Bring to the boil, then put the bonito fish in the pan and immediately turn off the heat. When the fish is beginning to sink, strain the sauce through a fine strainer or muslin or cheesecloth. Peel and grate the radish, put it on a *makisu* (bamboo blind) or in a fine sieve and allow the vegetable to drain naturally; do not squeeze it.

Cut the fish into fillets following the instructions for the *gomai oroshi* technique (see page 157), keeping the bones. Cut the fillets into 3-cm/$1\frac{1}{4}$-in squares and sprinkle with pepper. For the garnish, wash the asparagus and cut it from the tip into 7-cm/$2\frac{3}{4}$-in long pieces. Dry the spears on absorbent kitchen paper. Heat the oil for deep frying to 160 c/320 F. Fry the asparagus for 4 to 5 minutes, until it becomes clear green in colour. Drain and keep hot.

Coat the fish skeleton with flour, shaking off any excess. Dip it in the hot oil, bending the bones slightly. Hold the head with a fish slice [slotted spatula] and the tail with chopsticks. Place the bones, one at a time, in the oil, and fry for 10 to 12 minutes until they become crisp and easy to break (almost powdery). Drain on absorbent kitchen paper or on a wire rack, then keep the bones hot. Fry the remaining bones.

Coat the fish pieces with flour, shaking off any excess. Place the fish, four or five pieces at a time, in the hot oil and fry for 4 to 5 minutes, until crisp and light golden brown. Drain the fish on absorbent kitchen paper or on a wire rack; keep hot. Fry the remaining fish.

Line a serving plate with *tempura shikishi* or a white paper napkin. Put the bones on top and arrange the fish fillets on the bones. Garnish with the asparagus and lemon wedges. Pour the prepared dipping sauce into four small individual bowls and add the radish. The food should be eaten freshly cooked. **Serves 4**

**Note:** Small plates of Japanese soy sauce (about 1 tablespoon to each plate) can be served with the fish instead of the dipping sauce.

# Iwashi No Fry

—— *Fried Sprats* ——

| METRIC/IMPERIAL | AMERICAN |
|---|---|
| 350 g/12 oz sprats (about 10–11.5 cm/4–4½ in. in length) | ¾ lb sprats, smelts or other small oily fish (about 4–4½ in long) |
| pepper | pepper |
| 2 eggs | 2 eggs |
| 1 tablespoon milk | 1 tablespoon milk |
| plain flour for coating | flour for coating |
| breadcrumbs (page 159) | bread crumbs (page 159) |
| oil for deep frying | oil for deep frying |
| *Sauce* | *Sauce* |
| 4 tablespoons brown sauce | ¼ cup steak sauce |
| 3 tablespoons tomato ketchup | 3 tablespoons tomato ketchup |
| *Garnish* | *Garnish* |
| 1 lemon | 1 lemon |
| sprigs of parsley | sprigs of parsley |

Prepare the fish following the instructions for the *tebiraki* technique (see page 159) and sprinkle pepper on the fish. Beat the eggs thoroughly with the milk. Coat the fish with flour, shaking off any excess, then dip the fish in the beaten egg and coat it all over with the breadcrumbs, again shaking off any excess. Heat the oil for deep frying to 170 c/340 F. Place the fish, three or four at a time, in the hot oil and fry for 5 to 6 minutes, until cooked through and light golden brown. Drain the fish on absorbent kitchen paper or on a wire rack, then set aside and keep hot. Fry the remaining fish.

Mix the sauce ingredients in a small bowl, then pour it into four small individual plates. Arrange the cooked fish on a plate. Garnish with the lemon, cut into eight wedges, and the parsley. The food should be served as soon as it is cooked and the lemon is squeezed over the fish just before it is eaten. **Serves 4**

Opposite page: *Shabu Shabu (page 56)* **Overleaf**: *Moriawase (page 70)*

# Saba No Chukafu Miso Ni

*—— Mackerel with Miso ——*

| METRIC/IMPERIAL | AMERICAN |
|---|---|
| 2 mackerel | 2 mackerel |
| cornflour for coating | cornstarch for coating |
| 2 tablespoons oil plus oil for deep frying | 2 tablespoons oil plus oil for deep frying |
| 2 spring onions | 2 scallions |
| 40 g/1½ oz red *miso* | 3 tablespoons red *miso* |
| 1 tablespoon *sake* | 1 tablespoon *sake* |
| 2 teaspoons rice vinegar | 2 teaspoons rice vinegar |
| salt | salt |
| 300 ml/½ pint chicken stock | 1¼ cups chicken stock |
| 1 teaspoon sesame oil | 1 teaspoon sesame oil |
| 7 g/¼ oz fresh root ginger to garnish | ¼ oz fresh ginger root for garnish |

Clean the mackerel, then cut off their heads. Prepare the fish following the instruction for *san mai oroshi* technique (see page 158). Score the fish skin in a diamond pattern, then cut across the fillets into pieces measuring 3 cm/1¼ in wide. Coat the pieces of fish with cornflour [cornstarch], shaking off any excess.

Heat the oil for deep frying to 175 c/350 f. Lower the fish pieces, three or four at a time, into the hot oil and fry until crisp. It is not necessary to cook the fish right through. Drain the mackerel on absorbent kitchen paper or on a wire rack.

Remove the spring onion [scallion] roots and any bruised leaves, then wash and finely chop the rest. In a small bowl mix the *miso, sake*, rice vinegar and ½ teaspoon salt until smooth. Heat the 2 tablespoons oil in a frying pan. Stir-fry the chopped spring onions [scallions] for a few moments, then pour in the chicken stock and the *miso* mixture. Bring to the boil, then put the fish in the pan. Simmer gently until the sauce thickens, turning the fish over a few times and shaking the pan occasionally. Finally add the sesame oil.

Peel and slice the ginger thinly with the grain, then cut each slice thinly, again with the grain, into strips. Arrange the fish on a serving dish and sprinkle the ginger on top. The food should be served as soon as it is cooked.
**Serves 4**

*Top: Gyuniku Maki Age (page 76); bottom: Kara Age (page 73)*

# Moriawase

—— *Tempura* ——

(Illustrated on pages 66/67)

| METRIC/IMPERIAL | AMERICAN |
|---|---|
| *Dipping Sauce* | *Dipping Sauce* |
| 300 ml/½ pint *dashi* (page 153) | 1¼ cups *dashi* (page 153) |
| 4 tablespoons *mirin* | ¼ cup *mirin* |
| 4 tablespoons Japanese soy sauce | ¼ cup Japanese soy sauce |
| 5 g/¼ oz dried bonito fish | ¼ oz dried bonito fish |
| 10-cm/4-in piece large white radish | 4-in piece large white radish |
| *Seafood* | *Seafood* |
| 225 g/8 oz squid (the bigger and heavier the better) | ½ lb squid (the bigger and heavier the better) |
| 8 whole uncooked Mediterranean prawns | 8 raw jumbo shrimps |
| 1 red snapper | 1 red snapper |
| *Vegetables* | *Vegetables* |
| 1 green pepper | 1 green pepper |
| ½ sweet potato | ½ sweet potato |
| ½ aubergine (cut in half crossways and use the bottom part) | ½ eggplant (cut in half crossways and use the bottom part) |
| 4 medium cup mushrooms | 4 medium-size open cup mushrooms |
| 2 small onions | 2 small onions |
| *Batter* | *Batter* |
| 200 g/7 oz plain flour | 1¾ cups flour |
| pinch of salt | pinch of salt |
| 2 egg yolks | 2 egg yolks |
| oil for deep frying | oil for deep frying |

First make the *dipping sauce*: put all the ingredients except for the bonito fish and radish in a saucepan. Bring to the boil over a low to moderate heat, then add the bonito fish, and immediately turn off the heat. When the bonito fish is beginning to sink, strain the sauce into a bowl and discard the residue. Peel and grate the radish. Allow the grated radish to drain naturally in a sieve or on a bamboo blind; do not squeeze the vegetable.

Next prepare the seafood. Follow the squid preparation instructions under method 1 (see page 160). Wipe the squid with absorbent kitchen paper, then cut it into rectangles measuring 1.5 × 7 cm/¾ × 2¾ in. Remove the prawn [shrimp] heads and shells but leave the tail on. Use a cocktail stick to remove their veins. Lightly cut across the underside of the prawns [shrimp] in three or four places. Take off the red snapper's head, scrape off the scales and clean the inside of the fish. Cut up the fish in a *san mai oroshi* style following the instructions on page 158. Cut in half crossways and sprinkle with salt.
**Now prepare the vegetables:** cut the green pepper in half lengthways.

Remove the stalk, pith and seeds, then cut each half lengthways into four pieces. Peel and cut the sweet potato diagonally in 1-cm/½-in slices. Cut the stalk off the aubergine [eggplant] and quarter it lengthways. Soak the pieces in salted water for 15 minutes, removing any scum which rises to the surface. Drain and dry on absorbent kitchen paper. Make cuts 3 mm/⅛ in apart for three-quarters of the length of each piece of aubergine [eggplant]. Lightly press each aubergine [eggplant] quarter to make a fan shape. Wash the mushrooms and cut them in half. Peel the onions and cut them in half horizontally. Dry all the prepared ingredients thoroughly with absorbent kitchen paper, then coat them separately with flour, shaking off any excess.

To make the batter, start by sifting the flour twice; add a pinch of salt. Beat the egg yolks with about 400 ml/14 fl oz [2 cups] ice-cold water, then add the flour, stirring quickly until the flour is moistened and large lumps disappear. Do not stir too much, because the flour will become sticky. Add a little extra water if necessary to make a light batter.

Heat the oil for deep frying to 170 c/340 f. Fry vegetables first, then the seafood. Dip each of the vegetables into the batter, one piece at a time, then fry four or five pieces for about 2 to 3 minutes, or until light golden brown. Fry the seafood in the same way. Drain the fried food on absorbent kitchen paper or on a wire rack and keep it warm. Remove any scraps of batter from the pan while the *tempura* is frying.

Arrange the *tempura* attractively on individual plates, each one lined with *tempura shikishi* or a white paper napkin. Arrange some of the prepared radish on each plate. Pour the dipping sauce into small individual soup bowls, and divide the remaining radish between them before serving. Serve as soon as the food is cooked. **Serves 4**

**Note:** plain soy sauce can be served with the cooked *tempura* instead of the dipping sauce. The soy sauce should be poured into small individual plates, allowing 1 tablespoon to each.

# Sakanadango No Kikuka Age

—— *Fried Fishballs* ——

| METRIC/IMPERIAL | AMERICAN |
|---|---|
| 450 g/1 lb halibut | 1 lb halibut |
| 1 tablespoon *sake* | 1 tablespoon *sake* |
| salt | salt |
| 2 egg whites | 2 egg whites |
| 2 tablespoons cornflour | 2 tablespoons cornflour |
| 7 g/$\frac{1}{4}$ oz fresh root ginger | $\frac{1}{4}$ oz fresh ginger root |
| 25 g/1 oz dried *harusame* | $\frac{1}{4}$ cup dried *harusame* |
| plain flour for coating | flour for coating |
| oil for deep frying | oil for deep frying |
| *Garnish* | *Garnish* |
| 1 lemon | 1 lemon |
| 5-cm/2-in piece cucumber | 2-in piece cucumber |

Cut the fish following the *gomai oroshi* technique (see page 157), then mince [grind] it finely. Mix in the *sake*, a generous $\frac{1}{4}$ teaspoon salt, one egg white and cornflour [cornstarch]. Peel and grate the ginger then add it to the fish and mix thoroughly. Shape into 3-cm/1$\frac{1}{4}$-in diameter balls and place these on a plate.

Heat a steamer over a saucepan of boiling water. When the water is boiling rapidly, put the plate in the steamer. Put a tight-fitting lid on top and steam over a moderate heat for 10 to 15 minutes. Remove the plate from the steamer and allow to cool. Drain the fishballs on absorbent kitchen paper or a wire rack.

Break the *harusame* into 1-cm/$\frac{1}{2}$-in long pieces. Lightly whisk the remaining egg white. Coat the balls with flour shaking off any excess, then dip them into the egg white and coat with the *harusame*. Heat the oil for deep frying to 175 c/350 f. Lower the balls, three or four at a time, into the hot oil and fry for about 1 minute until the *harusame* becomes crisp. Drain the fishballs on absorbent kitchen paper or on a wire rack, keeping them hot until all the fishballs are cooked.

Cut the lemon into eight wedges. Cutting at a slant, slice the cucumber into 3-mm/$\frac{1}{8}$-in slices. Arrange the fishballs on a plate in an attractive layout with the garnish. The food should be eaten as soon as it is cooked and the lemon is squeezed over the fishballs just before they are eaten. **Serves 4**

# Kara Age

—— *Fried Chicken* ——

(Illustrated on page 68)

| METRIC/IMPERIAL | AMERICAN |
|---|---|
| 4 chicken leg joints | 4 chicken legs-with-thighs |
| cornflour for coating | cornstarch for coating |
| *Tsukejiru* | *Tsukejiru* |
| 4 tablespoons Japanese soy sauce | $\frac{1}{4}$ cup Japanese soy sauce |
| 4 tablespoons *sake* | $\frac{1}{4}$ cup *sake* |
| pepper | pepper |
| oil for deep frying | oil for deep frying |
| *Garnish* | *Garnish* |
| 1 lemon | 1 lemon |
| 10-cm/4-in piece cucumber | 4-in piece cucumber |

Prepare the chicken following the instructions on page 159 then cut it across into 3-cm/1$\frac{1}{4}$-in pieces. Mix the *Tsukejiru* ingredients in a bowl and add the chicken. Marinate for 20 to 30 minutes, turning the meat over a few times. Drain the chicken thoroughly on absorbent kitchen paper, then coat the pieces with cornflour [cornstarch], shaking off any excess.

For the garnish, cut the lemon into eight wedges and slice the cucumber at an angle into 3-mm/$\frac{1}{8}$-in wide pieces.

Heat the oil for deep frying to 160 c/320 f. Fry the chicken four or five pieces at a time for about 6 to 7 minutes, or until light golden brown. Drain the food on absorbent kitchen paper or on a wire rack, then keep it hot until all the pieces are cooked.

Arrange the chicken on a serving plate and garnish with lemon and cucumber. The food should be eaten as soon as it is cooked and the lemon is squeezed over the chicken just before it is eaten. **Serves 4**

# Toriniku Barei Maki

—— *Rolled Chicken with Potato* ——

(Illustrated on pages 86/87)

| METRIC/IMPERIAL | AMERICAN |
|---|---|
| 100 g/4 oz chicken breast | ¼ lb chicken breast |
| 2 to 3 medium potatoes | 2 to 3 medium-size potatoes |
| plain flour for coating | flour for coating |
| 1 small cucumber to garnish | 1 small cucumber for garnish |
| oil for deep frying | oil for deep frying |

Remove and discard the skin and bone from the chicken, then cut the meat against the grain into pieces measuring 4 cm/1½ in wide and 1 cm/½ in thick.

Peel the potatoes then cut them into very thick slices – 4 cm/1½ in thick. Discard the ends and retain the cylinder shaped pieces. Slice the potatoes in a *katsura muki* style (see page 164), so that you have long, curled strips. Soak the potatoes in water. Wipe the potatoes dry with absorbent kitchen paper. Open the strip carefully and brush the inside with flour. Roll a piece of the chicken inside each piece of potato. Secure with wooden cocktail sticks.

Prepare the cucumber for the garnish, cutting it into pieces following the *kirichigai* technique (see page 169).

Heat the oil for deep frying to 170 C/340 F. Coat the potato rolls with flour, shaking off any excess. Lower the rolls, several at a time, into the oil and fry for about 5 to 6 minutes, until cooked through and crisp. Drain the rolls on absorbent kitchen paper or a wire rack.

Sprinkle the hot rolls with salt and remove the cocktail sticks. Arrange the cooked potato rolls on small individual plates and garnish with the prepared cucumber. **Serves 4**

# Toridango No Teri Ni

*—— Minced [Ground] Chicken Balls ——*

| METRIC/IMPERIAL | AMERICAN |
| --- | --- |
| 1 egg | 1 egg |
| 3 chicken leg joints | 3 chicken legs-with-thighs |
| 2 teaspoons Japanese soy sauce | 2 teaspoons Japanese soy sauce |
| 2 teaspoons *mirin* or *sake* | 2 teaspoons *mirin* or *sake* |
| $\frac{1}{2}$ teaspoon salt | $\frac{1}{2}$ teaspoon salt |
| 2 tablespoons plain flour | 2 tablespoons flour |
| oil for deep frying | oil for deep frying |
| *Tare* | *Tare* |
| 4 tablespoons Japanese soy sauce | $\frac{1}{4}$ cup Japanese soy sauce |
| $4\frac{1}{2}$ teaspoons sugar | $4\frac{1}{2}$ teaspoons sugar |
| 2 tablespoons *sake* | 2 tablespoons *sake* |
| 1 small cucumber to garnish | 1 small cucumber for garnish |

Beat the egg thoroughly. Prepare the chicken following the instructions on page 159. Remove and discard the skin then mince [grind] the chicken meat finely. Thoroughly mix the meat with the beaten egg, the soy sauce, *mirin* or *sake*, salt and flour.

Heat the oil for deep frying to 170 c/340 f. Form the chicken mixture into small balls about 3 cm/$\frac{3}{4}$ in. in diameter. Roll a spoonful of the meat between two spoons to do this. Fry several balls at a time for 6 to 7 minutes, until cooked through and light golden brown. Repeat for the remaining meat. Drain the balls on absorbent kitchen paper or on a wire rack.

Put all the *tare* ingredients in a saucepan, bring to the boil, then reduce to a low to moderate heat. Put the chicken balls into the pan, then cook, shaking the pan gently and continuously, until most of the water has evaporated. Leave the balls in the pan to cool.

Thread the chicken balls on to eight 10-cm/4-in bamboo skewers. Cut the cucumber in a *kirichigai* style following the instructions on page 169. Arrange the skewered meatballs on small individual plates and add the garnish. **Serves 4**

# Gyuniku Maki Age

—— *Rolled Beef with Vegetables* ——

(Illustrated on page 68)

| METRIC/IMPERIAL | AMERICAN |
|---|---|
| 350 /12 oz good-quality fillet steak | $\frac{3}{4}$ lb boneless sirloin or other good- |
| 1 stick celery | quality steak |
| 3 fresh asparagus spears | 1 stalk celery |
| 6-cm/2$\frac{1}{2}$-in piece carrot | 3 fresh asparagus spears |
| 9–10 spring onions | 2$\frac{1}{2}$-in piece carrot |
| 3 sticks canned burdock | 9–10 scallions |
| 8 fresh mange-tout peas | 3 sticks canned burdock |
| *Dipping Sauce* | 8 snow or sugar peas |
| $\frac{1}{2}$ large white radish | *Dipping Sauce* |
| 300 ml/$\frac{1}{2}$ pint *dashi* (page 153) | $\frac{1}{2}$ large white radish |
| 100 ml/4 fl oz *mirin* | 1$\frac{1}{4}$ cups *dashi* (page 153) |
| 100 ml/4 fl oz Japanese soy sauce | $\frac{1}{2}$ cup *mirin* |
| 5 g/$\frac{1}{4}$ oz dried bonito fish | $\frac{1}{2}$ cup Japanese soy sauce |
| *Batter* | $\frac{1}{4}$ oz dried bonito fish |
| 120 g/4$\frac{3}{4}$ oz plain flour | *Batter* |
| pinch of salt | 1 cup flour |
| 1 egg yolk | pinch of salt |
| oil for deep frying | 1 egg yolk |
| | oil for deep frying |

Trim off and discard any fat from the meat, then place it in the freezer until half frozen. Slice the meat thinly against the grain. Trim the celery and remove any green leaves. Remove any coarse fibres then cut the celery into pieces measuring 6-cm/2$\frac{1}{2}$-in long and 5-mm/$\frac{1}{4}$-in wide. Wash the asparagus thoroughly in a few changes of water. Cut off any fibrous stalk ends. Cut the asparagus into 6-cm/2$\frac{1}{2}$-in long pieces and quarter them lengthways.

Peel the carrot and cut it lengthways into 5-mm/$\frac{1}{4}$-in wide slices. Remove the spring onion [scallion] roots and any bruised leaves, then wash and cut six or seven of the remainder into pieces measuring 6 cm/2$\frac{1}{2}$ in long. Finely chop the last two or three spring onions [scallions]. Cut the burdock sticks into 6-cm/2$\frac{1}{2}$-in long pieces and quarter these lengthways. Trim the mange-tout [snow] peas of stalks and any fibrous strings.

For the dipping sauce, peel and grate the radish then put it on a *makisu* (bamboo blind) or into a sieve and leave the vegetable to drain naturally. Do not squeeze the radish. Put all the remaining ingredients for the dipping sauce, except the bonito fish and radish, in a saucepan and bring to the boil, then immediately add the bonito fish to the pan. Turn off the heat; when the bonito fish is beginning to sink, strain the sauce through a sieve.

To make the batter, sift the flour twice. Beat the egg with 200 ml/7 fl oz [1 cup] ice cold water, then gradually stir in the flour and a pinch of salt until it is thoroughly moistened and the batter is smooth. Sprinkle flour on one side of each of the pieces of meat. Place three or four pieces of each of the vegetables (the celery, asparagus, carrot and burdock) on each slice of meat, then roll up firmly. Secure the rolls with wooden cocktail sticks.

Heat the oil for deep frying to 170 c/340 F. Fry the mange-tout [snow] peas for 1 to 2 minutes until they are clear in colour. Drain the peas on absorbent kitchen paper or on a wire rack, then keep them hot. Coat the meat rolls with flour, shaking off any excess, then dip them in the batter one at a time. Lower the rolls, two or three at a time, into the hot oil and fry for 6 to 7 minutes, until cooked through. Drain on absorbent kitchen paper or a wire rack, then keep hot and fry the remaining meat. make a cut at both ends of each roll, then halve them crossways. Take the cut sections of the meat rolls and stand them vertically on small individual plates. Garnish with the mange-tout [snow] peas.

Pour the dipping sauce into four small individual bowls, then add the radish and the chopped spring onions [scallions]. Serve this with the beef rolls. **Serves 4**

**Note:** you can serve soy sauce instead of the dipping sauce.

# Niku No Koromo Age

—— *Fried Beef* ——

| METRIC/IMPERIAL | AMERICAN |
|---|---|
| 450 g/1 lb topside or silverside | 1 lb flank steak |
| *Tsukejiru* | *Tsukejiru* |
| 7 g/$\frac{1}{4}$ oz fresh root ginger, peeled and grated | $\frac{1}{4}$ oz fresh ginger root |
| 2 tablespoons Japanese soy sauce | 2 tablespoons Japanese soy sauce |
| 2 tablespoons *sake* | 2 tablespoons *sake* |
| 2 teaspoons sesame oil | 2 teaspoons sesame oil |
| *Batter* | *Batter* |
| 1 egg | 1 egg |
| 4 tablespoons water | $\frac{1}{4}$ cup water |
| 4 tablespoons plain flour | $\frac{1}{4}$ cup flour |
| 4 tablespoons cornflour | $\frac{1}{4}$ cup cornstarch |
| 1 teaspoon baking powder | 1 teaspoon baking powder |
| oil for deep frying | oil for deep frying |
| *Garnish* | *Garnish* |
| 1 tomato | 1 tomato |
| sprigs of parsley | sprigs of parsley |

Trim off and discard any fat from the meat. Put the meat in the freezer until half frozen. Slice it thinly against the grain, cutting the pieces into 3-cm/1$\frac{1}{4}$-in squares. Mix all the *Tsukejiru* ingredients in a bowl. Mix the meat into the bowl. Leave to marinate for 10 to 15 minutes.

To make the batter, beat the egg with the water, then mix in the flour, cornflour [cornstarch] and baking powder until smooth. Add a little more water if necessary. Drain the meat and dry the pieces on absorbent kitchen paper, then add all the meat to the batter and mix thoroughly.

Heat the oil for deep frying to 170 C/340 F. Fry two or three pieces of the meat at a time for 2 to 3 minutes or until cooked through and crisp. Drain on absorbent kitchen paper or on a wire rack, then keep hot until all the meat is cooked.

Arrange the meat on a plate in an attractive layout. Garnish with the tomato, cut into eight wedges, and sprigs of parsley. **Serves 4**

# Butaniku No Tempura
—— *Pork Tempura* ——

| METRIC/IMPERIAL | AMERICAN |
|---|---|
| 450 g/1 lb boneless loin of pork | 1 lb boneless loin of pork |
| *Tsukejiru* | *Tsukejiru* |
| 20 g/$\frac{3}{4}$ oz fresh root ginger | $\frac{3}{4}$ oz fresh ginger root |
| 3 tablespoons Japanese soy sauce | 3 tablespoons Japanese soy sauce |
| pepper | pepper |
| *Batter* | *Batter* |
| 1 egg | 1 egg |
| 120 g/4$\frac{3}{4}$ oz plain flour | 1 cup flour |
| pinch of salt | pinch of salt |
| oil for deep frying | oil for deep frying |
| 1 small lettuce to serve | 1 small head lettuce to serve |
| 1 tomato to garnish | 1 tomato for garnish |
| *Sauce* | *Sauce* |
| 4 tablespoons Japanese soy sauce | 4 tablespoons Japanese soy sauce |
| 1 teaspoon dry mustard with a little water | 1 teaspoon dry mustard mixed with a little water |

Trim off and discard any fat from the meat and put it in the freezer until half frozen. Then slice it against the grain into pieces 2 mm/$\frac{1}{10}$ in thick. Cut into 5-cm/2-in squares.

Peel and grate the fresh root ginger. Mix all the ingredients for the *Tsukejiru* in a bowl. Add the meat, mix well and leave to marinate for 20 to 30 minutes.

To make the batter, beat the egg and 150 ml/$\frac{1}{4}$ pint [1 cup] ice-cold water together, then sift the flour and add it to the liquid with a pinch of salt. Stir quickly until the flour is moistened and any large lumps disappear.

Drain the meat on absorbent kitchen paper, then sprinkle flour on both sides of each slice. Heat the oil for deep frying to 170 c/340 f. Dip the meat into the batter, one piece at a time, then fry four or five pieces for about 3 to 4 minutes, or until cooked through and light golden brown. Drain the cooked meat on absorbent kitchen paper or on a wire rack, then keep hot until all the meat is cooked.

To serve, arrange the lettuce leaves around the edge of a serving platter and put the meat in the middle. Garnish with the tomato, cut into eight wedges.

Mix the ingredients for the sauce and pour it over the food. Alternatively divide the sauce between four small individual plates to serve with the meat. The food should be eaten as soon as it is cooked. **Serves 4**

# Abura Age Maki

—— *Fried Meat with Soya Bean Cake Roll* ——

(Illustrated on page 85)

| METRIC/IMPERIAL | AMERICAN |
|---|---|
| 3 *abura age* | 3 *abura age* |
| 1 onion | 1 onion |
| 3 dried *shiitake* | 3 dried *shiitake* |
| ½ carrot | ½ carrot |
| 1 tablespoon sesame oil | 1 tablespoon sesame oil |
| 1 tablespoon *sake* | 1 tablespoon *sake* |
| 2 teaspoons Japanese soy sauce | 2 teaspoons Japanese soy sauce |
| 1 tablespoon cornflour | 1 tablespoon cornstarch |
| 225 g/8 oz minced pork | ½ lb ground pork |
| salt | salt |
| 50 g/2 oz plain flour | ½ cup flour |
| *Sauce* | *Sauce* |
| 4 tablespoons Japanese soy sauce | ¼ cup Japanese soy sauce |
| 1 teaspoon dry mustard mixed with a little water | 1 teaspoon dry mustard mixed with a little water |
| oil for deep frying | oil for deep frying |
| *Garnish* | *Garnish* |
| bunch of spring onions | bunch of scallions |
| 1 small lettuce | 1 small head lettuce |

Make a cut in from three sides of the *abura age* leaving one of the long sides uncut. Open the *abura age* carefully without breaking the fourth side. Put a plate on top of the *abura age* to flatten it.

Peel the onion and cut it in half vertically, then slice it lengthways and chop finely crossways. Soak the dried *shiitake* in warm water for 20 minutes. Remove and discard the stems, then lightly squeeze the caps and slice them thinly. Finely chop the slices crossways. Following the instructions on page 163, cut the carrot in a *sengiri* style, then chop it finely. Mix the onion, *shiitake* and carrot with the sesame oil, *sake*, soy sauce, cornflour [cornstarch], pork and ½ teaspoon salt. Stir thoroughly.

Mix the flour with about 75 ml/3 fl oz [½ cup] water to make a smooth paste. For the garnish, remove the spring onion [scallion] roots and any bruised leaves, then wash and cut the rest into 4-cm/1½-in lengths and cut thinly lengthways. Soak in water for 5 to 10 minutes. Drain the spring onions [scallions] and toss in a sieve to remove the last of the water. Arrange some of the lettuce leaves around the edge of a big serving plate. Mix the sauce ingredients in a small bowl, then pour it into four small individual plates or set it aside to pour over the cooked food.

Lay out a *makisu* (bamboo blind) with the strands of wood running from left to right. Open one piece of *abura age* and lay it widthways with the outside surface on top. Coat the surface with a little paste, then spread about one-third of the mixed ingredients over two-thirds of the *abura age*. Roll the *abura age*, using the bamboo blind as a guide, then seal the edges and both sides with more of the paste. You may need to use quite a lot of the paste. Repeat for the remaining ingredients.

Heat the oil for deep frying to 160–165 c/320–330 f. Put a piece of the stuffed *abura age* on a fish slice [slotted spatula], with the end of the roll underneath. Dip the roll in the oil and leave it on the slice [spatula] for 30 seconds, then gently remove the fish slice [spatula]. Cook the stuffed *abura age* one or two at a time, for about 12 to 13 minutes, until cooked through and light golden brown. Drain on absorbent kitchen paper or on a wire rack, then keep hot until all the *abura age* are cooked. Slice each stuffed *abura age* into six pieces. Take the cut sections and stand them up on the plate, in a ring inside the lettuce. Arrange the remaining lettuce in the centre of the plate and put the spring onions [scallions] in the middle.

The food should be served as soon as it is cooked. Each person should use a leaf of lettuce to wrap a slice of *abura age* with some of the spring onions [scallions]. This is then eaten with the fingers. **Serves 4**

# Harumaki

—— *Chinese-style Spring Rolls* ——

(Illustrated on pages 86/87)

| METRIC/IMPERIAL | AMERICAN |
|---|---|
| 150 g/5 oz minced or finely chopped pork | 5 oz ground or finely chopped pork |
| 3 tablespoons Japanese soy sauce | 3 tablespoons Japanese soy sauce |
| 3 tablespoons *sake* | 3 tablespoons *sake* |
| 1 tablespoon cornflour | 1 tablespoon cornstarch |
| salt and pepper | salt and pepper |
| 1 (227-g/8-oz) can bamboo shoots | 1 (8-oz) can bamboo shoots |
| 1 carrot | 1 carrot |
| 2 spring onions | 2 scallions |
| 4 *kikurage* | 4 *kikurage* |
| 2 tablespoons plain flour | 2 tablespoons flour |
| $\frac{1}{4}$ cabbage | $\frac{1}{4}$ cabbage |
| 2 tablespoons sesame oil | 2 tablespoons sesame oil |
| 12 spring roll skins | 12 wonton skins |
| *Sauce* | *Sauce* |
| 4 tablespoons Japanese soy sauce | $\frac{1}{4}$ cup Japanese soy sauce |
| 1 teaspoon dry mustard mixed with a little water | 1 teaspoon dry mustard mixed with a little water |
| rice vinegar to taste (optional) | rice vinegar to taste (optional) |
| oil for deep frying | oil for deep frying |
| 1 tomato to garnish | 1 tomato for garnish |

Place the meat in a bowl and mix it with 2 tablespoons of the soy sauce, 2 tablespoons of the *sake*, the cornflour [cornstarch] and pepper to taste. Leave to marinate for 10 minutes.

Cut the bamboo shoots into 3-cm/1$\frac{1}{4}$-in wide slices, then cut them again to make fine strips – *sengiri* style (see page 163). Remove the spring onion [scallion] roots and any bruised leaves, then wash and cut the rest at a slant into 5-mm/$\frac{1}{4}$-in slices. Soak the dried *kikurage* in warm water for 20 minutes, remove and discard the stems, then lightly squeeze the mushroom caps. Cut into thin slices.

Make a paste from the flour by mixing it with 2 tablespoons water (or a little more) until smooth. Remove and discard the thicker stem parts of the cabbage, then shred the rest very thinly lengthways. This will produce individual strands of cabbage about 5-cm/2-in long. Soak the cabbage strands into salted water until the meat is ready.

Heat the sesame seed oil in a saucepan, add and stir-fry the pork until cooked. Add the bamboo shoots, carrots and *kikurage*, continue to stir well and fry for 1 minute. Add the remaining *sake* and soy sauce, $\frac{1}{2}$ teaspoon each of salt and pepper, then fry for another 30 seconds. Roughly divide the meat into 12 portions in the pan, then leave to cool.

Take an individual spring roll [*wonton*] skin, then place one portion of the mixture on to the middle of the skin. Roll up, sealing with the flour and water paste, following the diagrams.

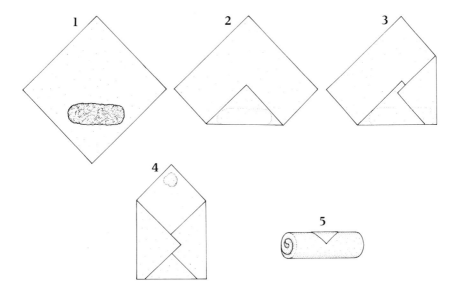

1 Place the meat mixture neatly in one corner of the spring roll [*wonton*] skin.
2 Fold the corner of the skin over the filling.
3 Fold the sides over the middle to enclose the filling completely.
4 Place a little of the flour and water paste on the remaining corner of pastry.
5 Roll up the filling, pressing the pasted corner neatly in place.

Mix all the ingredients together for the sauce and set it aside for later use. Heat the oil for deep frying to 170 C/340 F. Fry each roll until the skins are just brown and crisp. Drain the spring rolls on absorbent kitchen paper or a wire rack and keep hot while the remaining rolls are cooked.

Cut each roll at a slant into two, place these halves on the bed of shredded cabbage and garnish with the tomato, cut into fine wedges. Pour the sauce over the food or divide it between four individual plates. The food should be eaten hot, as soon as it is cooked, or cold. **Serves 4**

# Kushi Katsu

—— *Fried Pork Kebabs* ——

(Illustrated opposite)

| METRIC/IMPERIAL | AMERICAN |
|---|---|
| 225 g/8 oz fillet or boneless loin of pork | ½ lb boneless loin or tenderloin of pork |
| salt and pepper | salt and pepper |
| bunch of spring onions (those with thick stems are better) | bunch of scallions (those with thick stems are better) |
| 2 eggs | 2 eggs |
| 1 tablespoon milk | 1 tablespoon milk |
| plain flour for coating | flour for coating |
| Breadcrumbs (page 159) | Breadcrumbs (page 159) |
| oil for deep frying | oil for deep frying |
| *Sauce* | *Sauce* |
| 4 tablespoons brown sauce | ¼ cup steak sauce |
| 3 tablespoons tomato ketchup | 3 tablespoons tomato ketchup |
| *pepper to taste* | pepper to taste |
| *Garnish* | *Garnish* |
| 1 small cucumber | 1 small cucumber |
| 1 tomato | 1 tomato |

Trim off and discard any fat from the meat, then cut it into 2.5-cm/1-in cubes and sprinkle generously with salt and pepper. Remove the spring onion [scallion] roots and any bruised leaves, then wash and cut the rest in pieces measuring 3 cm/1¼ in long. Use the stem part only.

Thread three or four pieces of meat and three or four pieces of spring onion [scallion] alternately on to each of 12 (15-cm/6-in) bamboo skewers. Beat the eggs thoroughly with the milk. Coat the skewered meat with flour, dip the skewers in the beaten eggs and coat with breadcrumbs. Prepare the ingredients for the garnish. Cut the tomato into eight wedges; cut the cucumber following the *kirichigai* technique (see page 169).

Heat the oil for deep frying to 170 c/340 F. Fry the kebabs two or three at a time, in the oil for about 5 to 6 minutes, until cooked through and light golden brown on both sides. Drain the food on absorbent kitchen paper and keep hot until all are cooked.

Arrange three of the kebabs on each of four plates and garnish with the cucumber and tomato. Mix the ingredients for the sauce and pour it into small individual plates to serve. Alternatively the sauce can be poured straight over the kebabs. **Serves 4**

**Opposite page** *Top: Kushi Katsu; bottom: Abura Age Maki (page 80)*
**Overleaf** *Clockwise from top left: Toriniku Barei Maki (page 74), Moyashi No Wasabi Ae (page 43), Toridango No Teri Ni (page 75) and Harumaki (page 82)*

# Agedashi Dofu

—— *Fried Bean Curd* ——

(Illustrated opposite)

| METRIC/IMPERIAL | AMERICAN |
|---|---|
| 450 g/1 lb *tofu* | 1 lb *tofu* |
| cornflour for coating | cornstarch for coating |
| 3 spring onions | 3 scallions |
| 20 g/$\frac{3}{4}$ oz fresh root ginger (optional) | $\frac{3}{4}$ oz fresh ginger root (optional) |
| *Kake Jiru* | *Kake Jiru* |
| 400 ml/14 fl oz *dashi* (page 153) | 1$\frac{3}{4}$ cups *dashi* (page 153) |
| 4 tablespoons *mirin* | $\frac{1}{4}$ cup *mirin* |
| 4 tablespoons Japanese soy sauce | $\frac{1}{4}$ cup Japanese soy sauce |
| oil for deep frying | oil for deep frying |

Put the *tofu* on a chopping board, then tilt the board, resting it over a draining board or sink, to drain the *tofu* for 1 hour. Quarter the *tofu* and coat the pieces with cornflour [cornstarch], shaking off any excess, then leave to stand for a few minutes.

Remove the spring onion [scallion] roots and any bruised leaves, then wash and finely chop the rest. Peel and grate the ginger.

Put all the ingredients for the *kake jiru* in a saucepan. Bring to the boil, then immediately turn off the heat. The sauce can be heated up before serving, if necessary.

Heat the oil for deep frying to 170 c/340 f. Put a piece of the *tofu* on a fish slice [slotted spatula] and dip it in the oil, one piece at a time, then fry two or three pieces for about 4 to 5 minutes, until they are crisp and light golden brown.

Divide the *tofu* between four small individual bowls, pour the hot sauce over the *tofu* and sprinkle the ginger over, then top with the chopped spring onions [scallions]. Serve hot and eat with chopsticks or a spoon. **Serves 4**

*Top: Tamago Yaki (page 95); bottom: Agedashi Dofu*

# Kaki Age

—— *Fried Vegetables* ——

| METRIC/IMPERIAL | AMERICAN |
|---|---|
| 150 g/5 oz peeled cooked prawns or shrimps | 5 oz peeled cooked shrimp |
| salt | salt |
| 1 medium carrot | 1 medium-size carrot |
| 20 *mitsuba* or 6 spring onions | 20 *mitsuba* or 6 scallions |
| 1 medium onion | 1 medium-size onion |
| *Batter* | *Batter* |
| 1 egg | 1 egg |
| 107 g/4¼ oz plain flour | 1 cup flour |
| oil for deep frying | oil for deep frying |
| 4 tablespoons Japanese soy sauce | ¼ cup Japanese soy sauce |

Put the prawns or shrimps into boiling salted water. Bring back to the boil, then boil for 1 minute. Drain the prawns [shrimp] and toss them in a sieve to remove the last of the water.

Cut the carrot into very fine strips – *sengiri* style (see page 163). Wash the *mitsuba* and remove the roots, then cut them into 3-cm/1¼-in long pieces. If you are using the spring onions [scallions] remove their roots and any bruised leaves, then wash and cut the rest into pieces measuring 3 cm/1¼ in [⅔ cup] long. Peel the onion and cut it in half lengthways, then slice it thinly, again cutting in a lengthways direction.

Now make the batter: beat the egg with 100 ml/4 fl oz [⅔ cup] water in a mixing bowl. Sift the flour twice, then add it to the egg mixture with a pinch of salt. Stir quickly until the flour is moistened and there are no lumps in the batter.

Put all the prepared ingredients in the batter, then mix lightly. When you stir the ingredients in the bowl, the batter should just cover them. Heat the oil for deep frying to 170–180 c/340–350 f. Take a heaped spoonful of the ingredients, then transfer them to a slotted spoon one at a time and lower them gently into the oil. Hold the ingredients with chopsticks and keep each piece submerged for 30 seconds. Repeat with all the remaining ingredients, one at a time, then fry three or four pieces together for about 3 to 4 minutes, or until light golden brown. Drain the food on absorbent kitchen paper or on a wire rack, then keep it hot. Arrange the food on a plate lined with *tempura skikishi* or a white paper napkin.

Pour 1 tablespoon of the soy sauce into each of four small individual plates. The food should be eaten as soon as it is cooked and each piece dipped in the soy sauce. Add more soy sauce to the plates as necessary. **Serves 4**

# Cauliflower Ebi Koromo Age

—— *Fried Cauliflower with Prawns [Shrimp]* ——

| METRIC/IMPERIAL | AMERICAN |
|---|---|
| 350 g/12 oz fresh cauliflower | $\frac{3}{4}$ lb fresh cauliflower |
| 1 tablespoon lemon juice | 1 tablespoon lemon juice |
| 100 g/4 oz peeled cooked prawns or shrimps | $\frac{1}{4}$ lb peeled cooked shrimps |
| salt | salt |
| 1 egg | 1 egg |
| 1 teaspoon *sake* | 1 teaspoon *sake* |
| 50 g/2 oz plain flour plus 2 tablespoons for coating | $\frac{1}{2}$ cup flour plus 2 tablespoons flour for coating |
| oil for deep frying | oil for deep frying |
| 4 tablespoons Japanese soy sauce | $\frac{1}{4}$ cup Japanese soy sauce |

Divide the cauliflower into small florets, each about 3 cm/1$\frac{1}{4}$ in. in size. Put the cauliflower in a saucepan of boiling salted water, bring back to the boil, then boil for 1 minute. Drain the cauliflower, tossing it in a sieve or colander to remove the last of the water. Sprinkle the florets with the lemon juice.

To make the batter, start by cooking the shellfish: put the prawns [shrimp] in boiling salted water, bring back to the boil, then boil for 1 minute. Drain the prawns [shrimp], tossing them in a sieve to remove the last of the water. Mince [grind] the prawns [shrimp] coarsely.

Beat the egg thoroughly, then mix in the prawns [shrimp], *sake*, $\frac{1}{2}$ teaspoon salt and 3 tablespoons water. Sift the flour twice, then add it to the batter stirring thoroughly. Add a little more water if necessary.

Sprinkle the 2 tablespoons flour over the cauliflower, then put the florets in the batter and stir well. Heat the oil for deep frying to 170 c/340 f. Pick up the cauliflower in batter with a spoon, one piece at a time. Lower the pieces into the oil for 30 seconds, then gently remove the spoon. Fry four or five pieces at a time for about 3 to 4 minutes or until light golden brown. Drain the cauliflower on absorbent kitchen paper or on a wire rack and keep hot. Fry the remaining cauliflower.

Pour 1 tablespoon of the soy sauce into each of four small individual plates; serve this with the cauliflower. The food should be eaten as soon as it is cooked. **Serves 4**

# Itame Mono
## —— *Quick-fried Dishes* ——

These dishes are very simple to cook if you prepare everything beforehand. If you have a few different types of vegetables and some meat or seafood, you can prepare a substantial main dish. This type of dish is quite economical to prepare as all the cooking is very quick.

To ensure success, there are just a few points to remember. You should prepare all the ingredients before you begin cooking. The preparation is very important for these dishes. Cut most of the ingredients to the same size, so that they will cook evenly and look pleasing in the finished dish. Do not cook the food for too long, otherwise the ingredients will become too soft. Try to retain the natural textures of the ingredients.

## Kanitama
### —— *Chinese-style Fried Egg and Crab* ——

| METRIC/IMPERIAL | AMERICAN |
|---|---|
| 2 spring onions | 2 scallions |
| 2 dried *shiitake* or 2 mushrooms | 2 dried *shiitake* or fresh mushrooms |
| 4–5 eggs | 4–5 eggs |
| salt and pepper | salt and pepper |
| 1 (250-g/8¾-oz) can crab meat, drained | 1 (8-oz) can crabmeat, drained |
| 2 tablespoons lard | 2 tablespoons lard |
| *Amazu An* | *Amazu An* |
| 200 ml/7 fl oz chicken stock | 1 cup chicken stock |
| 2 tablespoons Japanese soy sauce | 2 tablespoons Japanese soy sauce |
| 3 tablespoons rice vinegar | 3 tablespoons rice vinegar |
| 5 teaspoons sugar | 5 teaspoons sugar |
| 2 teaspoons cornflour mixed with a little water | 2 teaspoons cornstarch mixed with a little water |
| 2 tablespoons shelled peas to garnish | 2 tablespoons shelled peas for garnish |

Remove the spring onion [scallion] roots and any bruised leaves, then wash and chop the rest finely. Soak the dried *shiitake* in warm water for 20 minutes. Remove their stems and lightly squeeze the caps, then thinly slice these lengthways. If you use fresh mushrooms, slice them thinly.

For the garnish, put the peas into boiling salted water, bring back to the boil, then boil for 2 minutes. Remove the pan from the heat and trickle water into the pan until the peas are cool. This method of cooling the peas will avoid wrinkled skins.

Beat the eggs with $\frac{1}{2}$ teaspoon salt and pepper to taste, then add all the crab meat, breaking it up slightly, the spring onions [scallions] and the *shiitake* or fresh mushrooms and mix thoroughly.

Heat a frying pan, put in the lard and allow it to become hot. When the fat is smoking hot pour in the egg mixture and stir briskly for a few moments. Reduce the heat to moderate, then allow the eggs to set. Use a large fish slice [slotted spatula] to turn the set egg, being careful not to break it. Fry for a few minutes on the second side.

Put all the *Amazu An* ingredients except the cornflour [cornstarch] mixture into a saucepan. Add the peas, bring to the boil, then reduce the heat. Give the cornflour [cornstarch] mixture a stir, then pour it into the pan, stirring continuously.

Cut up the set egg mixture into seven pieces following diagram 1, then arrange the pieces on a serving platter following diagrams 2 and 3, laying portion 7 on top of the other pieces. Pour the hot sauce over and serve.
**Serves 4**

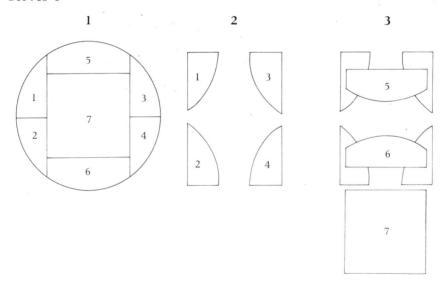

# Okonomi Yaki

—— *Pancakes* ——

(Illustrated on page 105)

| METRIC/IMPERIAL | AMERICAN |
|---|---|
| 225 g/8 oz cabbage | $\frac{1}{2}$ lb cabbage |
| 10-cm/4-in piece Japanese yam | 4-in piece Japanese yam |
| 65 g/1$\frac{1}{2}$ oz plain flour | 6 tablespoons flour |
| 225 g/8 oz minced beef | $\frac{1}{2}$ lb ground beef |
| 4 eggs | 4 eggs |
| *Choose from the following topping ingredients:* | *Choose from the following topping ingredients:* |
| 225 g/8 oz squid | $\frac{1}{2}$ lb squid |
| 225 g/8 oz rump steak, sliced thinly against the grain | $\frac{1}{2}$ lb boneless sirloin steak, sliced thinly against the grain |
| 225 g/8 oz boneless loin of pork, sliced thinly against the grain | $\frac{1}{2}$ lb boneless loin of pork, sliced thinly against the grain |
| 225 g/8 oz peeled cooked prawns | $\frac{1}{2}$ lb peeled cooked shrimps |
| *Garnish* | *Garnish* |
| 3 spring onions | 3 scallions |
| *benishoga* (red ginger pickles) | *benishoga* (red ginger pickles) |
| 5 g/$\frac{1}{4}$ oz dried bonito fish | $\frac{1}{4}$ oz dried bonito fish |
| oil for cooking | oil for cooking |
| *Sauces (choose your favourite)* | *Sauces (choose your favourite)* |
| 1 4 tablespoons brown sauce mixed with 2 tablespoons tomato ketchup | 1 $\frac{1}{4}$ cup steak sauce mixed with 2 tablespoons tomato ketchup |
| 2 Japanese soy sauce | 2 Japanese soy sauce |
| 3 tomato ketchup | 3 tomato ketchup |

Following the instructions on page 163, cut the cabbage into fine strips – *sengiri* style. Peel and grate the yam. Sift the flour into a bowl, then beat in 100 ml/4 fl oz [$\frac{2}{3}$ cup] water. Add the beef, the cabbage and the yam and beat thoroughly. Add the eggs to the mixture, stirring well, to make a thick batter.

If you are using the squid, prepare it following the instructions for method 1 on page 160, then cut it into oblong pieces measuring 5 × 2 cm/2 × $\frac{3}{4}$ in.

For the garnish, remove the spring onion [scallion] roots and any bruised leaves, then wash and finely chop the rest. Slice the *benishoga* thinly with the grain, then cut them thinly, again with the grain, to make strips. Put all the garnishing ingredients on a plate, keeping the ingredients separate.

Heat 1 tablespoon oil in a frying pan. Take a large spoonful of the batter mixture, then pour it into the pan to make a pancake measuring about 12 cm/4$\frac{1}{2}$ in. in diameter. Spread the mixture into a circle using the base of the spoon. Reduce the heat to low or moderate. Put some of your chosen ingredients (the steak, pork, prawns [shrimp] or squid) on top of the pancake and sprinkle with some of the garnishing ingredients. Pour just a little extra batter on top of the pancake and put a lid on the pan. Fry for about 10 minutes until the top of the pancake becomes slightly dry, then turn it over. Put the lid back, then fry for a further 5 to 6 minutes. Finally, turn the pancake over again and pour 1 tablespoon of your chosen sauce on top. Serve at once. **Serves 4**

**Note:** depending on the size of your pan you should be able to cook three or four pancakes at a time. If you have a table heater, then cook the pancakes at the table.

# Tamago Yaki

—— *Rolled Omelette* ——

(Illustrated on page 88)

| METRIC/IMPERIAL | AMERICAN |
|---|---|
| 2 spring onions | 2 scallions |
| 4 eggs | 4 eggs |
| $4\frac{1}{2}$ teaspoons Japanese soy sauce | $4\frac{1}{2}$ teaspoons Japanese soy sauce |
| 3 tablespoons oil | 3 tablespoons oil |
| 1 small cucumber to garnish | 1 small cucumber for garnish |

For the garnish, cut the cucumber following the instructions for the *kiri chigai* technique (see page 169). Trim the spring onions [scallions], then wash and finely chop them. Beat the eggs with the spring onions [scallions] and the soy sauce.

Heat 1 tablespoon of the oil in a frying pan. Pour half the beaten eggs into the pan and reduce the heat to moderate. Tilt the pan until the eggs cover the bottom evenly then allow them to half set. Roll up the omelette, then move it to one end of the pan. Pour in half the remaining oil, heat through then pour in half the remaining egg and cook as before. When half set roll the cooked omelette with the half set egg to make a large roll. Move the roll to one side of the pan. Repeat once more for the remaining egg, to make a large omelette roll.

Cut the rolled eggs across into quarters, then cut each quarter diagonally in half again. Take the cut sections of the eggs and stand them up on the flat side on a serving dish with the garnish. **Serves 4**

# Tori No Teriyaki

—— *Grilled [Pan-Broiled] Chicken* ——

(Illustrated on pages 106/107)

| METRIC/IMPERIAL | AMERICAN |
|---|---|
| 2 chicken leg joints | 2 chicken legs-with-thighs |
| *Tare* | *Tare* |
| 2 tablespoons *sake* | 2 tablespoons *sake* |
| 3 tablespoons Japanese soy sauce | 3 tablespoons Japanese soy sauce |
| $4\frac{1}{2}$ teaspoons sugar | $4\frac{1}{2}$ teaspoons sugar |
| 2 tablespoons oil for cooking | 2 tablespoons oil for cooking |
| *Garnish* | *Garnish* |
| 1 small lettuce | 1 small head lettuce |
| 1 tomato | 1 tomato |

Prepare the chicken following the instructions on page 00, then use a fork to pierce the skin of the chicken in several places. Mix the *tare* ingredients in a bowl and add the meat, then mix well. Set aside to marinate for 30 minutes, turning the meat over occasionally. Remove the meat and reserve the *tare*. Heat a heavy-based saucepan, pour in the oil and allow it to become hot. Put the chicken in the pan with the skin side underneath. Reduce to a low or moderate heat and fry for 4 to 5 minutes. Turn the meat over and fry for another 2 to 3 minutes. Pour the *Tare* into the pan and bring to the boil, then reduce the heat and put a lid on the pan. Simmer gently for 5 to 6 minutes, turning the meat over a few times. Finally, when there is still some *tare* left in the pan, increase the heat and boil until most of the liquid has evaporated. Do not allow the sauce to burn and shake the pan continuously to prevent this. Leave to cool.

To serve, remove the chicken meat from the pan and cut it across into 1-cm/$\frac{1}{2}$-in wide pieces. Arrange the lettuce leaves around the edge of a serving plate. Cut the tomato into eight wedges. Arrange the chicken on the plate and add the tomato to garnish. Serve cold.

# Niku No Tamago Tsukeyaki

###### —— *Korean-style Fried Beef with Egg* ——

| METRIC/IMPERIAL | AMERICAN |
|---|---|
| 450 g/1 lb rump steak or silverside | 1 lb flank steak |
| salt and pepper | salt and pepper |
| plain flour for coating | flour for coating |
| 2 eggs | 2 eggs |
| oil for cooking | oil for cooking |
| *Garnish* | *Garnish* |
| 10-cm/4-in piece cucumber | 4-in piece cucumber |
| 1 tomato | 1 tomato |
| 4 tablespoons Japanese soy sauce to serve (optional) | $\frac{1}{4}$ cup Japanese soy sauce for serving (optional) |

Trim off and discard any fat from the meat. Place it in the freezer until half frozen and slice it against the grain about 5 mm/$\frac{1}{4}$ in thick. Cut the meat into pieces about 5 cm/2 in square. Sprinkle salt and pepper generously on both sides of the meat, then set it aside for 10 to 15 minutes. For the garnish, cut the cucumber at a slant into 2-mm/$\frac{1}{10}$-in slices. Cut the tomato lengthways into eight wedges.

Coat the meat with flour, shaking off any excess. Beat the eggs thoroughly. Heat a frying pan, pour in 2 tablespoons oil. You should pour in extra oil as necessary during cooking. Set the heat to low or moderate, dip the meat one piece at a time into the beaten egg, then fry four or five pieces together for about 2 to 3 minutes. Turn over and fry the second side for another 1 to 2 minutes or until cooked through and light golden brown. Cook the remaining meat, keeping the cooked pieces hot until all the food is prepared.

Arrange the meat on a serving plate so that the pieces overlap each other. Add the garnishing ingredients then serve at once. If you like, pour 1 tablespoon of the soy sauce into each of four small individual plates and serve this with the meat. **Serves 4**

# Gyoza

—— *Chinese-style Fried Meat Dumpling* ——

(Illustrated on pages 106/107)

| METRIC/IMPERIAL | AMERICAN |
|---|---|
| *Dough* | *Dough* |
| 120 g/4¾ oz strong plain flour | 1 cup strong bread flour |
| 75 g/3 oz plain flour | ¾ cup all-purpose flour |
| salt and pepper | salt and pepper |
| *Filling* | *Filling* |
| 3 Chinese leaves | 3 leaves *bok choy* |
| 2 dried *shiitake* | 2 dried *shiitake* |
| 2 spring onions | 2 scallions |
| 1 clove garlic | 1 clove garlic |
| 7 g/¼ oz fresh root ginger | ¼ oz fresh ginger root |
| 225 g/8 oz minced pork | ½ lb ground pork |
| 2 tablespoons Japanese soy sauce | 2 tablespoons Japanese soy sauce |
| 1 tablespoon *sake* | 1 tablespoon *sake* |
| 1 teaspoon sesame oil | 1 teaspoon sesame oil |
| 1 tablespoon cornflour | 1 tablespoon cornstarch |
| 2 tablespoons oil for cooking | 2 tablespoons oil for cooking |
| *Dipping Sauce* | *Dipping Sauce* |
| 4 tablespoons Japanese soy sauce | ¼ cup Japanese soy sauce |
| 4 teaspoons sesame oil | 4 teaspoons sesame oil |

First make the dough: sift both types of flour together twice with a pinch of salt. Make a well in the flour, then pour in about 100 ml/4 fl oz [⅔ cup] warm water little by little, kneading it into the flour with your hand. Do not make the dough too sticky or too dry: it should be just moist to the touch. Cover with a damp cloth and leave the dough to stand for 1 hour.

Turn the dough out on to a working surface and knead it for 4 to 5 minutes, sprinkling the surface with flour as required. The dough will become soft and moist. Make a 2.5-cm/¾-in diameter roll from the dough, then cut it into 2-cm/¾-in lengths. Roll each piece into a small ball, then knead and flatten the balls in the palm of your hand. Each skin should be about 6–7 cm/2½–3 in. in diameter. Sprinkle flour on the dough as necessary.

For the filling, wash the Chinese leaves [*bok choy*] then cut them lengthways into thin shreds and chop these crossways. Lightly squeeze the pieces to remove any water. Soak the dried *shiitake* in warm water for 20 minutes. Remove their stems, then lightly squeeze the caps and cut them into thin slices. Chop these slices crossways. Remove the spring onion [scallion] roots and any bruised leaves, then wash and finely chop the rest. Peel and chop the garlic and the ginger.

Mix all the filling ingredients, except the Chinese leaves [*bok choy*], thoroughly with $\frac{1}{2}$ teaspoon salt, the soy sauce, *sake*, sesame oil and cornflour [cornstarch]. Lastly add the leaves and mix gently.

Take a piece of *gyoza* skin in the left hand and put 1 teaspoonful of the pork mixture on the dough – the filling should cover about one-third of the dough. Use your right hand to fold up and seal the dough over the middle of the filling similar to a small Cornish pasty [turnover]. Pinch the dough between your thumb and index finger to seal it properly.

Have ready some boiling water. Heat a frying pan and pour in the oil. Allow the oil to become hot, then put the dumplings close together in two rows in the pan and fry for 1 minute. Very carefully pour in enough boiling water to come halfway up the *gyoza*. Reduce the heat to a low setting then put a lid on the pan and simmer gently for 20 to 25 minutes. If there is still some water left at the end of this time, increase the heat and boil until most of the water has evaporated but do not allow the food to burn.

Mix the soy sauce and sesame oil for the dipping sauce and divide it between four small individual plates to serve with the *gyoza*. Arrange the *gyoza* close together on a plate and serve hot – each person should help themselves. **Makes 30 to 35**

**Note:** the filled, uncooked *gyoza* can be frozen but they should not be frozen after cooking. The frozen *gyoza* can be cooked as above, there is no need to defrost them first.

# Shoga Yaki

—— *Fried Pork with Ginger* ——

| METRIC/IMPERIAL | AMERICAN |
| --- | --- |
| 450 g/1 lb boneless loin of pork | 1 lb boneless loin of pork |
| *Tsukejiru* | *Tsukejiru* |
| 20 g/¾ oz fresh root ginger | ¾ oz fresh ginger root |
| 4 tablespoons *sake* | ¼ cup *sake* |
| 3 tablespoons Japanese soy sauce | 3 tablespoons Japanese soy sauce |
| 1½ tablespoons mirin | 1½ tablespoons mirin |
| 1 tablespoon oil for cooking | 1 tablespoon oil for cooking |
| *Garnish* | *Garnish* |
| 1 tomato | 1 tomato |
| 1 large stick celery (with leaves) | 1 large stalk celery (with leaves) |

Trim off and discard any fat from the meat, then slice it against the grain into 5-mm/¼-in thick pieces. Peel and grate the ginger, then put it in a bowl with the other *Tsukejiru* ingredients. Add the meat, mix well and leave to marinate for 10 to 15 minutes.

Prepare the ingredients for the garnish: cut the tomato into eight wedges. Cut the celery into 3-cm/1¼-in lengths, then cut each piece lengthways into fine strips. Place the strips of celery into cold water until you are ready to garnish the dish and drain them at the last minute.

Remove the meat from the marinade, then lay out the pieces on absorbent kitchen paper to dry them thoroughly. Reserve the *Tsukejiru* for later use. Heat a frying pan, pour in the oil and allow it to become hot. Fry the meat until both sides are light brown, then reduce to a low heat until the meat is cooked. Do not allow the meat to burn. Remove the meat from the pan, then pour in the reserved *Tsukejiru*. Bring to the boil, then simmer gently for 1 minute. Replace the meat in the pan and simmer until most of the liquid has evaporated, turning the meat over occasionally to prevent burning.

To serve, remove the meat from the pan and cut it across into 3-cm/1¼-in wide pieces. Arrange the meat on small individual plates, then add the tomato and celery to garnish. The food should be eaten as soon as it is cooked.
**Serves 4**

# Jagaimo To Niku Itame

*—— Fried Potato and Meat ——*

(Illustrated on pages 106/107)

| METRIC/IMPERIAL | AMERICAN |
|---|---|
| 4 medium potatoes | 4 medium-size potatoes |
| 1 carrot | 1 carrot |
| 225 g/8 oz boneless loin of pork | $\frac{1}{2}$ lb boneless loin of pork |
| 2 tablespoons cornflour | 2 tablespoons cornstarch |
| 4 tablespoons oil | $\frac{1}{4}$ cup oil |
| 1 tablespoon Japanese soy sauce | 1 tablespoon Japanese soy sauce |
| salt and pepper | salt and pepper |
| *Tsukejiru* | *Tsukejiru* |
| 2 tablespoons Japanese soy sauce | 2 tablespoons Japanese soy sauce |
| 2 tablespoons *sake* | 2 tablespoons *sake* |

Peel and thinly slice the potatoes, then soak them in water for a few minutes. Following the instructions on page 163, cut the potatoes into fine strips – *sengiri* style. Soak the strips in water. Peel the carrot and cut it into strips similar in size to the potatoes. Trim off and discard any fat from the meat, then place it in the freezer until half frozen. Cut the meat against the grain into 1-cm/$\frac{1}{2}$-in slices. Cut these lengthways into thin strips. Mix the *Tsukejiru* ingredients in a bowl and add the meat. Mix well, then leave to marinate for 10 to 15 minutes. Drain the meat and sprinkle the cornflour [cornstarch] over the pieces.

Heat a frying pan, pour in half the oil and stir-fry the meat. When the meat is cooked remove it from the pan and set aside for later use. Pour the remaining oil into the pan, allow it to become hot, then add the vegetables. Add the soy sauce, 1 teaspoon salt and pepper to taste, then continue to stir-fry until the vegetables are tender.

Finally, put the meat back in the pan and stir-fry for 1 minute. Transfer the food to a serving plate, arranging it so that the individual ingredients show distinctly. The food should be eaten as soon as it is cooked. **Serves 4**

# Yasai Itame

###### —— *Fried Vegetables* ——

(Illustrated on pages 106/107)

| METRIC/IMPERIAL | AMERICAN |
|---|---|
| 1 (227-g/8-oz) can bamboo shoots | 1 (8-oz) can bamboo shoots |
| 1 carrot | 1 carrot |
| 225 g/8 oz fresh bean sprouts | $\frac{1}{2}$ lb bean sprouts (about 4 cups) |
| 100 g/4 oz cooked ham | $\frac{1}{4}$ lb cooked ham |
| 5 spring onions | 5 scallions |
| 2 tablespoons oil | 2 tablespoons oil |
| 2 tablespoons Japanese soy sauce | 2 tablespoons Japanese soy sauce |
| salt and pepper | salt and pepper |

Cut the bamboo shoots across into 4-cm/1$\frac{1}{2}$-in slices, then slice each piece thinly lengthways. Peel and thinly slice the carrot, cutting at a slant. Put the bean sprouts in a sieve then wash them under running water. Drain thoroughly tossing them in the sieve to remove the last of the water. Cut the ham into oblong pieces measuring 4 × 1 cm/1$\frac{1}{2}$ × $\frac{1}{2}$ in. Remove the spring onion [scallion] roots and any bruised leaves, then wash and cut the rest into 4-cm/1$\frac{1}{2}$-in lengths.

Heat a saucepan, pour in the oil and heat it through. Put all the prepared ingredients in the pan, then stir-fry for 30 seconds. Add the soy sauce, $\frac{1}{2}$ teaspoon salt and pepper to taste. Stir-fry for a further 1 to 1$\frac{1}{2}$ minutes. Transfer the food to a serving dish, arranging each ingredient to show distinctly. The food should be eaten as soon as it is cooked. **Serves 4**

**Note:** you can add other types of vegetables, prawns [shrimp], meat or eggs to this basic recipe.

# Mushi Mono

## —— *Steamed Dishes* ——

Steaming food allows the ingredients to cook evenly, it keeps the full flavour in the food and it keeps the ingredients at their best in terms of appearance. Remember the following points and your cooking will be successful.

When steaming foods you can't remove any scum or very strong flavours and smells, so use fresh, plain-flavoured ingredients which are not too watery. Put the ingredients in the steamer only when there is plenty of steam coming from the pan. Keep the pan topped up with boiling water during cooking. If you want to prevent condensation dripping on the food, then wrap a clean cloth around the lid so that it sits between the lid and the steamer. When steaming eggs, do not cover the pan too tightly and use a low setting to make sure they cook evenly.

## Mushi Tamago

### —— *Steamed Egg* ——

| METRIC/IMPERIAL | AMERICAN |
|---|---|
| 2 spring onions | 2 scallions |
| 4 eggs | 4 eggs |
| 2 tablespoons Japanese soy sauce | 2 tablespoons Japanese soy sauce |

Remove the spring onion [scallion] roots and any bruised leaves, then wash and finely chop the rest. Beat the eggs thoroughly with the chopped spring onions [scallions], add 200 ml/7 fl oz [1 cup] water and the soy sauce, then pour the mixture into a small saucepan.

Bring to the boil, then stir for 30 seconds. Put a lid on the pan and reduce to a low heat, then simmer gently for 10 to 12 minutes, or until the eggs are just set. Transfer the eggs to small individual bowls and serve hot. **Serves 4**

# Wakadori No Sakamushi

*—— Steamed Chicken ——*

| METRIC/IMPERIAL | AMERICAN |
|---|---|
| 3 chicken leg joints | 3 chicken legs-with-thighs |
| *Tsukejiru* | *Tsukejiru* |
| 100 ml/4 fl oz *sake* | ½ cup *sake* |
| salt | salt |
| *Dipping Sauce* | *Dipping Sauce* |
| 4 tablespoons Japanese soy sauce | ¼ cup Japanese soy sauce |
| 1 teaspoon dry mustard mixed with | 1 teaspoon dry mustard mixed with |
| a little water | a little water |
| *Garnish* | *Garnish* |
| 1 small cucumber | 1 small cucumber |
| 1 lemon | 1 lemon |

Prepare the chicken following the instructions on page 159. Pierce the skin with a fork in several places. For the *Tsukejiru*, mix the *sake* with 100 ml/4 fl oz [½ cup] water and ½ teaspoon salt. Put the chicken meat into the bowl, mix well and leave to marinate for 10 minutes, turning occasionally. Heat a steamer; when there is plenty of steam put the bowl in the steamer. Put a lid on top and seal it tightly. Steam the chicken over a moderate heat for 15 to 20 minutes or until cooked through. Remove the bowl from the steamer and leave the meat to cool in the *Tsukejiru*. Prepare the cucumber for the garnish following the *kirichigai* technique (see page 169).

Drain the chicken and dry it on absorbent kitchen paper. Remove and discard the skin then slice the meat against the grain into 5-mm/¼-in wide pieces. Arrange the meat attractively on a serving plate and garnish with the lemon, cut into eight wedges and the cucumber. For the dipping sauce mix the soy sauce and mustard then divide it between four small individual plates. **Serves 4.**

**Opposite page** *Okonomi Yaki (page 94)* **Overleaf** *Clockwise from top left: Tori No Teriyaki (page 96), Gyoza (page 98), Jagaimo To Niku Itame (page 101) and Yasai Itame (page 102)*

# Hiyashi Dori

—— *Chicken Salad* ——

(Illustrated opposite)

| METRIC/IMPERIAL | AMERICAN |
| --- | --- |
| 2 chicken leg joints | 2 chicken legs-with-thighs |
| salt | salt |
| 2 tablespoons *sake* | 2 tablespoons *sake* |
| $\frac{1}{2}$ cucumber | $\frac{1}{2}$ cucumber |
| 100 g/4 oz *tofu* | $\frac{1}{4}$ lb *tofu* |
| 2 tomatoes | 2 tomatoes |
| *Karashi Joyu* | *Karashi Joyu* |
| 4 tablespoons Japanese soy sauce | $\frac{1}{4}$ cup Japanese soy sauce |
| 1 teaspoon dry mustard mixed with a little water | 1 teaspoon dry mustard mixed with a little water |

Prepare the chicken following the instruction on page 159, then use a fork to pierce the skin several times. Sprinkle 1 teaspoon salt and the *sake* on both sides of the chicken meat, then leave it to marinate for 10 minutes.

Heat a steamer, when there is plenty of steam, put the chicken in a suitable dish and stand it in the steamer. Put a tight-fitting lid on top and steam the chicken over a moderate heat for 15 to 20 minutes, or until cooked through. Remove the dish from the steamer and leave to cool.

Drain the chicken and dry it on absorbent kitchen paper then remove and discard the skin. Cut the chicken into 2-cm/$\frac{3}{4}$-in cubes. Cut the cucumber in half lengthways, then cut it an angle into 3-mm/$\frac{1}{8}$-in thick slices. Quarter the *tofu*. Cut the tomatoes in half vertically, then cut them into 5-mm/$\frac{1}{4}$-in slices crossways.

To serve, put the *tofu* in the centre of a serving dish then arrange all the other ingredients attractively around it. Mix the soy sauce and mustard for the sauce, then divide it between four small individual plates to serve with the salad. **Serves 4**

*Top: Hiyashi Dori; bottom: Nikudango No Tamago Mabushi (page 111)*

# Chawan Mushi

*—— Steamed Egg with Chicken ——*

<table>
<tr><td align="center">METRIC/IMPERIAL</td><td align="center">AMERICAN</td></tr>
<tr><td align="center">600 ml/1 pint dashi (page 153)</td><td align="center">2½ cups dashi (page 153)</td></tr>
<tr><td align="center">4 teaspoons Japanese soy sauce</td><td align="center">4 teaspoons Japanese soy sauce</td></tr>
<tr><td align="center">1 teaspoon mirin</td><td align="center">1 teaspoon mirin</td></tr>
<tr><td align="center">salt</td><td align="center">salt</td></tr>
<tr><td align="center">3 eggs</td><td align="center">3 eggs</td></tr>
<tr><td align="center">4 whole Mediterranean prawns</td><td align="center">4 jumbo shrimp</td></tr>
<tr><td align="center">1 chicken leg joint</td><td align="center">1 chicken leg-with-thigh</td></tr>
<tr><td align="center">4 button mushrooms</td><td align="center">4 button mushrooms</td></tr>
<tr><td align="center">4 mitsuba or 1 spring onion</td><td align="center">4 mitsuba or 1 scallion</td></tr>
<tr><td align="center">Garnish</td><td align="center">Garnish</td></tr>
<tr><td align="center">piece of lemon peel measuring<br>5 × 2 cm/2 × ¾ in</td><td align="center">piece of lemon peel measuring<br>2 × ¾ in</td></tr>
</table>

Heat the *dashi* in a saucepan then add 1 tablespoon of the soy sauce, the *mirin* and ½ teaspoon salt. Make sure the salt is fully dissolved, then leave to cool. It is very important that the *dashi* is cool before continuing with the recipe.

Beat the eggs thoroughly, then beat in the *dashi*. Strain the mixture through a fine strainer or clean muslin or cheesecloth. Remove the heads and shells from the prawns [shrimp], leaving the tails on, then remove the veins with a cocktail stick. Prepare the chicken following the instructions on page 00, then cut the meat against the grain into 2-cm/¾-in wide pieces. Mix the chicken meat with the remaining soy sauce and set it aside to marinate for 10 minutes. Wash the mushrooms and cut them in half.

Remove and discard the *mitsuba* roots and leaves, then wash the stems. Cut these into 1.5-cm/¾-in pieces. If you are using spring onion [scallion], remove their roots and any bruised leaves, then wash and chop the rest finely.

For the garnish cut the lemon peel into 5-mm/¼-in squares. Arrange all the prepared ingredients except the *mitsuba* in individual custard cups or small bowls. Top up with the egg mixture until the cups are about four-fifths full. Put the *mitsuba* on top. Use a small spoon to remove any bubbles.

Heat a steamer; when there is plenty of steam put the cups in the steamer. Wrap a cloth around the lid of the steamer, then put it on but do not seal it too tightly. After 2 minutes reduce the heat to a low setting and steam for 20 to 25 minutes. To check if the food is cooked, pierce the centre of each portion with a cocktail stick. If the juice runs out clear the eggs are cooked. Garnish with lemon peel squares and serve hot; eat with small spoons. **Serves 4**

# Nikudango No Tamago Mabushi

—— *Steamed Meatballs* ——

(Illustrated on page 108)

| METRIC/IMPERIAL | AMERICAN |
|---|---|
| $\frac{1}{2}$ (227-g/8-oz) can bamboo shoots | $\frac{1}{2}$ (8-oz) can bamboo shoots |
| 1 spring onion | 1 scallion |
| 1 dried *shiitake* | 1 dried *shiitake* |
| 50 g/2 oz peeled cooked prawns or shrimps | 2 oz peeled cooked shrimp |
| 2 eggs | 2 eggs |
| 225 g/8 oz minced pork | $\frac{1}{2}$ lb ground pork |
| 1$\frac{1}{2}$ teaspoons Japanese soy sauce | 1$\frac{1}{2}$ teaspoons Japanese soy sauce |
| 1 teaspoon sesame oil | 1 teaspoon sesame oil |
| salt | salt |
| 2 tablespoons cornflour plus extra for coating | 2 tablespoons cornstarch plus extra for coating |
| *Dipping Sauce* | *Dipping Sauce* |
| 4 tablespoons Japanese soy sauce | $\frac{1}{4}$ cup Japanese soy sauce |
| 1 tablespoon rice vinegar | 1 tablespoon rice vinegar |
| sprigs of parsley to garnish | sprigs of parsley for garnish |

Following the instructions on page 163, cut the bamboo shoots in a *sengiri* style then chop finely crossways. Remove the spring onion [scallion] roots and any bruised leaves, then wash and finely chop the rest. Soak the dried *shiitake* in warm water for 20 minutes. Remove and discard the stems and lightly squeeze the caps. Slice these thinly, then chop them finely. Roughly chop the prawns [shrimp]. Boil one of the eggs for 12 minutes, then soak it in cold water until cool. Cut the egg in half and separate the white and yolk. Press each separately through a sieve. Lightly beat the remaining egg.

Thoroughly mix the minced pork with the beaten egg, the soy sauce, sesame oil, $\frac{1}{2}$ teaspoon salt and the cornflour [cornstarch]. Shape this mixture into 2.5-cm/1-in diameter meatballs. Do this by rolling a spoonful of the meat between two spoons. Coat the balls with cornflour [cornstarch].

Brush the base of a steamer with oil, then set it over a pan of boiling water. Wrap a cloth around the lid of the steamer. Put the meatballs on the bottom of the steamer, allowing a little space between each one. When plenty of steam builds up, put the lid on and steam the meatballs for 15 to 20 minutes.

Arrange the meatballs on a serving plate and garnish each one with a little of the sieved egg white and yolk. Add parsley sprigs to complete the garnish.

Mix the soy sauce and rice vinegar for the dipping sauce, then pour it into four small individual plates. The meatballs should be served freshly cooked and the dipping sauce accompanies them. **Serves 4**

# Ni Mono

## *—— Boiled Food ——*

Steamed rice and *sake* complement the dishes in this chapter and this combination forms a common part of the average Japanese meal. In this type of cooking it is important to use the correct method of preparation for each ingredient and to add the flavours in the correct order. Always use the freshest possible ingredients. When you cook seafood, boil the stock first, add the flavouring, then put in the seafood. If the seafood is added to cold water lots of the flavour will be lost and the delicate flesh will break up easily.

## Iwashi No Korean Style Nikomi
### *—— Boiled Sardines with Garlic ——*

| METRIC/IMPERIAL | AMERICAN |
|---|---|
| 20 fresh sardines (about 10–11.5-cm/4–4$\frac{1}{2}$-in. in length) | 20 fresh sardines (about 4–4$\frac{1}{2}$-in. long) |
| 2 cloves garlic | 2 cloves garlic |
| 100 ml/4 fl oz Japanese soy sauce | $\frac{1}{2}$ cup Japanese soy sauce |
| $\frac{1}{2}$ teaspoon chilli powder | $\frac{1}{2}$ teaspoon chili powder |
| pepper | pepper |
| 1 small cucumber to garnish | 1 small cucumber for garnish |

Clean the fish and remove their heads (or ask your fishmonger to do this for you). Wash thoroughly, then cut the tails off. Peel and grate or crush the garlic, then mix it with the soy sauce, 100 ml/4 fl oz [$\frac{1}{2}$ cup] water, the chilli powder and pepper to taste in a saucepan. Put the fish in the pan, bring to the boil, then simmer gently until most of the liquid has evaporated. Baste the fish continuously with the sauce as it cooks.

Meanwhile, prepare the cucumber for the garnish following the *kirichigai* technique (see page 169). Arrange five sardines on each of four small individual plates and garnish with cucumber. Serve at once. **Serves 4**

# Ika No Shoyu Ni

—— *Boiled Squid with Soy Sauce* ——

<table>
<tr><td>METRIC/IMPERIAL</td><td>AMERICAN</td></tr>
<tr><td>legs and flaps from 225 g/8 oz squid –<br>use the trimmings from the squid<br>cooked in Tempura (page 70)</td><td>tentacles and flaps from $\frac{1}{2}$ lb squid –<br>use the trimmings from the squid<br>cooked in Tempura (page 70)</td></tr>
<tr><td>2 spring onions</td><td>2 scallions</td></tr>
<tr><td>2–3 tablespoons Japanese soy sauce</td><td>2–3 tablespoons Japanese soy sauce</td></tr>
<tr><td>pepper</td><td>pepper</td></tr>
</table>

Cut the squid legs [tentacles] into pieces measuring 3-cm/1$\frac{1}{4}$-in long. Cut the gills into pieces measuring the same as the legs. Remove the spring onion [scallion] roots and any bruised leaves, then wash and cut the rest into 3-cm/1$\frac{1}{4}$-in lengths.

Put the prepared squid and the spring onions [scallions] in a small saucepan. Add the soy sauce and pepper to taste, then bring to the boil. Reduce the heat and cover the pan, then simmer for 10 to 15 minutes or until most of the liquid has evaporated. Stir well.

To serve, arrange the squid and the spring onions [scallions] on a small plate or in a bowl. **Serves 4**

# Gyuniku No Tsukudani

—— *Boiled Beef* ——

<table>
<tr><td align="center">METRIC/IMPERIAL</td><td align="center">AMERICAN</td></tr>
<tr><td align="center">225 g/8 oz silverside or topside</td><td align="center">½ lb flank steak</td></tr>
<tr><td align="center">50 g/2 oz fresh root ginger</td><td align="center">2 oz fresh ginger root</td></tr>
<tr><td align="center">2 tablespoons sake</td><td align="center">2 tablespoons sake</td></tr>
<tr><td align="center">3 tablespoons sugar</td><td align="center">3 tablespoons sugar</td></tr>
<tr><td align="center">7 teaspoons Japanese soy sauce</td><td align="center">7 teaspoons Japanese soy sauce</td></tr>
<tr><td align="center">pepper</td><td align="center">pepper</td></tr>
<tr><td align="center">20 g/¾ oz fresh root ginger to garnish</td><td align="center">¾ oz fresh ginger root for garnish</td></tr>
</table>

Trim off and discard any fat from the meat. Place the meat in the freezer until half frozen, then slice it thinly against the grain and cut the slices into 3-cm/1¼-in squares. Peel and slice the 50 g/2 oz ginger thinly with the grain.

Prepare the garnish: slice the ginger thinly with the grain, then cut each slice with the grain into thin strips. Soak the ginger strips in water for 1 to 2 minutes, then drain them in a sieve and set aside until the dish is served.

Pour 4 tablespoons water into a saucepan, then add the 50 g/2 oz ginger, *sake* and the sugar. Bring to the boil and put the meat in the pan. Bring back to the boil, then reduce the heat to low or moderate. Stir for 1 minute, then add the soy sauce and pepper to taste. Simmer gently until most of the liquid has evaporated.

To serve, arrange the meat on small individual plates and arrange the ginger garnish on top. The food should be eaten as soon as it is served, or it can be allowed to cool completely, then served cold. **Serves 4**

# Nikujaga

*—— Beef with Potatoes ——*

| METRIC/IMPERIAL | AMERICAN |
|---|---|
| 4–5 medium potatoes | 4–5 medium-size potatoes |
| 225 g/8 oz rump steak | $\frac{1}{2}$ lb boneless sirloin steak |
| 1 onion | 1 onion |
| 3 tablespoons oil | 3 tablespoons oil |
| 100 ml/4 fl oz *sake* | $\frac{1}{2}$ cup *sake* |
| 2 tablespoons *mirin* | 2 tablespoons *mirin* |
| 3 tablespoons sugar | 3 tablespoons sugar |
| 4 tablespoons Japanese soy sauce | $\frac{1}{4}$ cup Japanese soy sauce |
| 2 tablespoons shelled peas to garnish | 2 tablespoons shelled peas for garnish |

Peel and quarter the potatoes, then soak them in water for 10 to 15 minutes. Trim off and discard any fat from the meat. Place it in the freezer until half frozen, then slice it thinly against the grain. Cut the pieces into 3-cm/1$\frac{1}{4}$-in squares. Peel the onion and cut it lengthways into eight wedges.

For the garnish, put the peas in boiling salted water, bring back to the boil, then boil for 2 minutes. Trickle cold water into the pan until the peas become cool – this method of cooking the peas ensures that they do not have wrinkled skins.

Heat a heavy-based saucepan, then pour in the oil, allow the oil to become hot, then stir-fry the meat and the onion and reduce the heat to moderate. When the meat is cooked add the potato and continue to stir-fry until the potatoes become translucent. Pour in 400 ml/14 fl oz [1$\frac{3}{4}$ cups] water, the *sake* and *mirin*. Add the sugar and bring to the boil, then simmer gently for 10 minutes. Add the soy sauce to the pan, stir gently and simmer until half the liquid has evaporated. Check the potatoes with a wooden cocktail stick or skewer, and when they are cooked add the peas. Increase the heat and cook until most of the liquid has evaporated, shaking the pan to prevent the ingredients from sticking.

To serve, put the food in small individual bowls, arranging the ingredients so that they are all showing. The food should be served as soon as it is cooked. Alternatively it can be cooled and chilled thoroughly first. **Serves 4**

# Gobo To Gyuniku No Nitsuke

*—— Boiled Burdock and Beef ——*

| METRIC/IMPERIAL | AMERICAN |
|---|---|
| 100 g/4 oz fresh or canned burdock | $\frac{1}{4}$ lb fresh or canned burdock |
| 225 g/$\frac{1}{2}$ lb silverside or topside | $\frac{1}{2}$ lb flank steak |
| 10 *mitsuba* or 2 spring onions | 10 *mitsuba* or 2 scallions |
| 7 g/$\frac{1}{4}$ oz fresh root ginger | $\frac{1}{4}$ oz fresh ginger root |
| 2 teaspoons oil | 2 teaspoons oil |
| 2 eggs, beaten | 2 eggs, beaten |
| *Sauce* | *Sauce* |
| 200 ml/7 fl oz *dashi* (page 153) | 1 cup *dashi* (page 153) |
| 100 ml/4 fl oz *mirin* | $\frac{1}{2}$ cup *mirin* |
| 100 ml/4 fl oz Japanese soy sauce | $\frac{1}{2}$ cup Japanese soy sauce |
| 5 teaspoons *sake* | 5 teaspoons *sake* |
| 2 tablespoons sugar | 2 tablespoons sugar |

If you are using fresh burdock, then clean it with a scrubbing brush under running water, removing any bruised parts. Peel the fresh burdock. Using a sharp knife, slice the burdock thinly and put it in a bowl of water (see *sasagaki* technique, page 164). Rinse the burdock, then leave it to soak in fresh water until all the other ingredients are ready.

Trim off and discard any fat from the meat then slice it thinly against the grain. Cut the slices into 3-cm/1$\frac{1}{4}$-in squares. Remove and discard the *mitsuba* roots and leaves, then wash the rest and cut it into 3-cm/1$\frac{1}{4}$-in lengths. If you are using spring onions [scallions], remove their roots and any bruised leaves, then wash and cut the rest into 3-cm/1$\frac{1}{4}$-in lengths and shred these thinly lengthways. Peel and slice the ginger thinly with the grain, then cut the slices into thin strips, again cutting with the grain. Soak the strips in water. Drain the burdock in a sieve or colander.

Heat the oil in a saucepan and stir-fry the meat until it changes colour. Reduce the heat to moderate, add the burdock to the pan and stir-fry for 2 to 3 minutes. Increase the temperature and pour all the sauce ingredients into the pan. Add the ginger, bring to the boil, then add the *mitsuba*. Reduce to a moderate heat and stir in the beaten eggs. Stir gently once, then when the eggs are half set, turn off the heat.

Serve the ingredients in small individual bowls, arranging the food so that all the ingredients show distinctly. The food should be eaten as soon as it is cooked. **Serves 4**

# Wakatake Ni

—— *Boiled Bamboo Shoots* ——

| METRIC/IMPERIAL | AMERICAN |
|---|---|
| 2 (227-g/8-oz) cans bamboo shoots (whole or half bamboo shoots) | 3 (8-oz) cans bamboo shoots (whole or half bamboo shoots) |
| 7 g/$\frac{1}{4}$ oz dried *wakame* | $\frac{1}{4}$ oz dried *wakame* |
| *To cook the bamboo shoots* | *To cook the bamboo shoots* |
| 800 ml/27 fl oz *dashi* (page 153) | 3 cups *dashi* (page 153) |
| 7 g/$\frac{1}{4}$ oz dried bonito fish | $\frac{1}{4}$ oz dried bonito fish |
| 100 ml/4 fl oz *sake* | $\frac{1}{2}$ cup *sake* |
| 3 tablespoons *mirin* | 3 tablespoons *mirin* |
| 1 tablespoons sugar | 1 tablespoon sugar |
| 4 tablespoons Japanese soy sauce | $\frac{1}{4}$ cup Japanese soy sauce |
| salt | salt |
| *To cook the wakame* | To cook the *wakame* |
| 100 ml/4 fl oz dashi (page 153) | $\frac{1}{2}$ cup *dashi* (page 153) |
| 2 teaspoons *mirin* or *sake* | 2 teaspoons *mirin* or *sake* |
| 2 teaspoons Japanese soy sauce | 2 teaspoons Japanese soy sauce |

Cut the bamboo shoots across into 1.5-cm/$\frac{3}{4}$-in slices. Put the bamboo shoots in a saucepan. From the ingredients listed to cook the bamboo shoots, pour in the *dashi* and add the bonito fish, then bring to the boil and reduce the heat to a low setting. Add the *sake, mirin* and sugar to the pan, then simmer gently for 5 to 6 minutes. Finally add the soy sauce and 1 teaspoon salt and simmer for a further 10 minutes. Turn off the heat and leave to cool.

Soak the *wakame* in water for 5 to 10 minutes. Drain the *wakame* and add it to a saucepan of boiling water, then drain it immediately and put into cold water to cool. Drain the *wakame* in a sieve and cut it across into 3-cm/1$\frac{1}{4}$-in wide pieces. If the whole piece of *wakame* is not very big, then you may have to cut smaller pieces.

Put all the ingredients listed for cooking the *wakame* into a saucepan. Bring to the boil, then add the *wakame* to the pan, bring back to the boil and turn off the heat. Leave to cool.

Drain the bamboo shoots and the *wakame*, reserving both lots of cooking liquid. Arrange both vegetables separately in individual dishes, then pour in a little of each stock. Serve cool. **Serves 4**

# Renkon No Jigatsuo Ni

—— *Lotus Roots with Bonito Fish* ——

(Illustrated on page 125)

| METRIC/IMPERIAL | AMERICAN |
|---|---|
| 12-cm/4½-in piece fresh or canned lotus root | 4½-in piece fresh or canned lotus root |
| 1 tablespoon rice vinegar | 1 tablespoon rice vinegar |
| 5 g/¼ oz dried bonito fish | ¼ oz dried bonito fish |
| 2 tablespoons sugar | 2 tablespoons sugar |
| 3 tablespoons Japanese soy sauce | 3 tablespoons Japanese soy sauce |
| 3-cm/1¼-in piece cucumber to garnish | 1¼-in piece cucumber for garnish |

Peel the lotus root and cut away the sides to produce a flower shape. Slice the lotus root across into 1-cm/½-in thick pieces. Put these in a bowl with enough cold water to cover them and add the rice vinegar. Leave to soak for 30 minutes, removing any scum which rises to the surface of the water.

For the garnish, cut the cucumber following the instructions for the *sen roppon* technique (see page 163). Soak the cucumber in water for 1 minute, then drain thoroughly and set aside.

Drain and rinse the lotus roots with fresh water and put them into a saucepan. Pour in 600 ml/1 pint [2½ cups] water and add the bonito fish. Bring to the boil, then simmer gently for 7 to 8 minutes. Add the sugar and continue to simmer for 4 to 5 minutes. Finally add the soy sauce, then simmer gently until the sauce reduces to half its original volume. Turn the lotus roots over carefully during cooking.

Serve the lotus roots in small individual bowls and sprinkle the cucumber on top. The food should be eaten as soon as it is cooked, or it can be allowed to cool completely, then served cold. **Serves 4**

# Gomoku Mame

—— *Boiled Soya Beans* ——

(Illustrated on page 125)

| METRIC/IMPERIAL | AMERICAN |
|---|---|
| 150 g/5 oz dried soya beans | 1 cup dried soybeans |
| 50 g/2 oz *konnyaku* | 2 oz *konnyaku* |
| 3-cm/1¼-in piece canned lotus root | 1¼-in piece canned lotus root |
| ½ carrot | ½ carrot |
| 100 g/4 oz canned burdock | ¼ lb canned burdock |
| 5-cm/2-in square *kombu* | 2-in square *kombu* |
| 600 ml/1 pint *dashi* (page 153) | 2½ cups *dashi* (page 153) |
| 1 tablespoon sugar | 1 tablespoon sugar |
| 1 tablespoon *mirin* | 1 tablespoon *mirin* |
| 3 tablespoons Japanese soy sauce | 3 tablespoons Japanese soy sauce |

Soak the soya beans overnight in plenty of cold water. Cut the *konnyaku* and lotus root into 1-cm/½-in cubes. Quarter the carrot and burdock lengthways, then cut it into 5-mm/¼-in thick slices. Wipe the *kombu* on absorbent kitchen paper and cut it into 5-mm/¼-in squares (you will find that kitchen scissors are the best implement to use for this).

Drain the soya beans and place them in a saucepan. Pour in fresh water – about three times the volume of the beans. Bring to the boil, then cover the pan and boil gently until the beans are tender – about 1 hour. Top up the water as necessary. Drain the cooked beans and soak them in cold water until cool, then remove their husks.

Put the beans in a saucepan and add the *dashi*. Add the prepared ingredients, then bring to the boil and simmer gently 10 minutes. Add the sugar and the *mirin* to the pan, simmer gently for 2 to 3 minutes. Finally add the soy sauce, then simmer until most of the water (about eighty percent) has evaporated.

Arrange the beans in neat mounds in four small individual bowls and pour some of the cooking liquid over them. The food should be eaten as soon as it is cooked, or it can be allowed to cool and served cold. **Serves 4**

# Yaki Mono

## *—— Grilled [Broiled] and Baked Dishes ——*

The essential characteristics of these dishes is that they are all cooked by high heat – over an open heat, under a grill [broiler] or in a hot oven – to retain the full flavour of the food and to further enhance it by the additional flavour which the cooking method imparts.

This method of cooking food is very simple – you can prepare meat, vegetables or dried foods by this method – but there is little margin for error. As a guide, remember to cook the ingredients under a very hot grill [broiler] whenever the recipe states this requirement and try to keep the space between the food and the heat source quite even. Cook the side which is going to be served uppermost for the greatest part of the time – allow about sixty percent of the cooking time for this side. And remember always to preheat the grill [broiler] before cooking the food.

## Amadai Kogane Yaki

### *—— Grilled [Broiled] Sea Bream ——*

(Illustrated on pages 126/127)

| METRIC/IMPERIAL | AMERICAN |
|---|---|
| 1 medium sea bream | 1 medium-size sea bream, porgy or |
| salt | scup |
| 3-cm/1¼-in piece carrot | salt |
| 2 dried *kikurage* | 1¼-in piece carrot |
| 10 *mitsuba* | 2 dried *kikurage* |
| 2 eggs plus 4 egg yolks | 10 *mitsuba* |
| ½ teaspoon *sake* | 2 eggs plus 4 egg yolks |
| ½ teaspoon *mirin* | ½ teaspoon *sake* |
| ½ teaspoon Japanese soy sauce | ½ teaspoon *mirin* |
| 50 g/2 oz peeled cooked prawns or | ½ teaspoon Japanese soy sauce |
| shrimps | 2 oz peeled cooked shrimps |
| *Garnish* | *Garnish* |
| 5-cm/2-in piece cucumber | 2-in piece cucumber |
| small piece of turnip | small piece of turnip |
| a little rice vinegar | a little rice vinegar |

Clean and scale the fish. Remove its head, then rinse it thoroughly. Alternatively ask your fishmonger to clean and scale the fish. Prepare the fish following the instructions for the *sanmai oroshi* technique (see page 158). Remove any remaining bones using clean tweezers if necessary. Sprinkle salt on both sides of the fillets and put the fish on a large plate or baking tray. Tilt the plate or tray to drain for $1\frac{1}{2}$ hours. Rinse the fish under running water and dry it on absorbent kitchen paper.

Peel and prepare the carrot following the instructions for the *sengiri* technique (see page 163). Soak the dried *kikurage* in warm water for 20 minutes, then drain and thinly slice them.

Remove and discard the roots and leaves from the *mitsuba*, then wash and cut the rest into 3-cm/$1\frac{1}{4}$-in lengths.

For the garnish, cut the cucumber at a slant into fine slices. Prepare the turnip following the instructions for *kikuka giri* (page 169). Soak in ice-cold water with a little rice vinegar added until you are ready to serve the fish.

Beat the egg yolks with the whole eggs in a saucepan. Mix in the *sake*, *mirin* and soy sauce then add the carrot and *kikurage*. Heat the pan over a low to moderate heat, stirring well until the eggs are half set; do not overcook the eggs. Turn off the heat, add the *mitsuba* and prawns [shrimp] to the pan, then leave to cool.

Thread the four portions of fish on to eight long metal skewers as shown in the diagram. Cook the fish under a hot grill [broiler] until cooked and crisp. Transfer the fish to a large ovenproof dish putting it skin side uppermost and remove the skewers gently. Divide the egg mixture between the pieces of fish, then bake in a hot oven (220 c, 425 f, gas 7) until just brown on top – about 15 minutes.

Arrange the cooked fish on small individual plates and garnish with the cucumber and turnip flower shape. The food should be eaten as soon as it is cooked. **Serves 4**

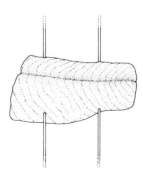

# Saba No Korean Style Yaki

—— *Grilled Mackerel* ——

| METRIC/IMPERIAL | AMERICAN |
|---|---|
| 1 large mackerel | 1 large mackerel |
| 1 tablespoon sesame seeds, lightly roasted | 1 tablespoon sesame seeds, lightly roasted |
| *Tare* | *Tare* |
| 1 clove garlic | 1 clove garlic |
| 7 g/$\frac{1}{4}$ oz fresh root ginger | $\frac{1}{4}$ oz fresh ginger root |
| 2 spring onions | 2 scallions |
| 4 tablespoons Japanese soy sauce | $\frac{1}{4}$ cup Japanese soy sauce |
| 1 tablespoon *sake* | 1 tablespoon *sake* |
| 1 teaspoon chilli powder | 1 teaspoon chili powder |
| *Garnish* | *Garnish* |
| 1 tomato | 1 tomato |
| sprigs of watercress | sprigs of watercress |

Clean the fish and cut off its head, then rinse it thoroughly. Alternatively, ask your fishmonger to do this for you. Prepare the mackerel following the instructions for the *sanmai oroshi* technique (see page 158), then cut it into four portions.

For the *tare* peel and grate the garlic and the ginger. Remove the spring onion [scallion] roots and any bruised leaves, then wash and finely chop the rest. Mix all these ingredients with the soy sauce, *sake* and chilli powder in a bowl. Put the mackerel in the bowl, and leave it to marinate for 1 hour, turning the fish over a few times.

Place the mackerel on a rack brushed with oil. Cook under a preheated grill [broiler] for 3 to 4 minutes, then reduce the heat to low or moderate. Carefully turn the fish over and sprinkle sesame seeds on top, then grill [broil] for another 2 to 3 minutes until cooked through and crisp. Take care not to burn the fish.

To serve, put the mackerel on small individual plates and garnish with the tomato cut into eight wedges and watercress. The food should be served as soon as it is cooked. **Serves 4**

**Note:** you can use small haddock fillets instead of the mackerel in this recipe. Omit the ginger, and use a pan instead of the rack. Grill [broil] for 30 seconds on one side, then turn the fish over gently. Grill [broil] for 4 to 5 minutes, or until it is cooked through and crisp.

# Toriniku Namba Maki

—— *Rolled Chicken* ——

(Illustrated on pages 126/127)

METRIC/IMPERIAL

2 chicken leg joints
6 spring onions
*Tsukejiru*
$4\frac{1}{2}$ teaspoons Japanese soy sauce
$1\frac{1}{2}$ teaspoons *sake*
3 tablespoons *mirin*
1 teaspoon lemon juice
1 tomato to garnish

AMERICAN

2 chicken legs-with-thighs
6 scallions
*Tsukejiru*
$4\frac{1}{2}$ teaspoons Japanese soy sauce
$1\frac{1}{2}$ teaspoons *sake*
3 tablespoons *mirin*
1 teaspoon lemon juice
1 tomato for garnish

Prepare the chicken following the instructions on page 159. Mix all the *tsuke-jiru* ingredients in a shallow dish or a small roasting pan. Put the chicken in the dish or pan and leave it to marinate for 30 minutes, turning occasionally. Remove the spring onion [scallion] roots and any bruised leaves, then wash and cut the onions across in half.

Cut two 20-cm/8-in squares of cooking foil and brush them with a little oil. Lay one piece of chicken on the foil, with the skin side underneath. Put half of the spring onions [scallions] on top; use the foil as a guide to roll up the chicken tightly. Fold the edges of the foil over to enclose the meat, sealing it well. Repeat with the remaining chicken. Cook the chicken in a hot oven (220 c, 425 f, gas 7) for 25 to 30 minutes. Leave to cool.

Remove the foil and cut the chicken into 1-cm/$\frac{1}{2}$-in wide slices. Cut the tomato into eight wedges. Arrange these on small individual plates, garnish with the tomato and serve cold. **Serves 4**

# Yakitori

—— *Chicken Kebabs* ——

(Illustrated on pages 126/127)

| METRIC/IMPERIAL | AMERICAN |
|---|---|
| 450 g/1 lb chicken breasts | 1 lb chicken breasts |
| bunch of spring onions | bunch of scallions |
| *Tare* | *Tare* |
| 200 ml/7 fl oz Japanese soy sauce | 1 cup Japanese soy sauce |
| 3 tablespoons sugar | 3 tablespoons sugar |
| 2 cloves garlic | 2 cloves garlic |
| 7 g/$\frac{1}{4}$ oz fresh root ginger | $\frac{1}{4}$ oz fresh ginger root |
| *Garnish* | *Garnish* |
| 1 small cucumber | 1 small cucumber |
| 1 tomato | 1 tomato |

Remove the skin and any bone from the chicken, then cut the meat into cubes measuring 1.5 × 2.5 cm/$\frac{3}{4}$ × 1 in. Remove the spring onion [scallion] roots and any bruised leaves, then wash and cut the root ends into 3-cm/$1\frac{1}{4}$-in lengths. Thread the meat and the spring onions [scallions] alternately on to eight 15-cm/6-in bamboo skewers. Each skewer should have about four or five pieces each of meat and onion.

Mix the soy sauce and sugar for the *tare* in a small roasting tin [pan] or shallow dish. Peel and grate the garlic and ginger, then add these to the soy sauce mixture. Lay the kebabs in the dish or tin [pan] and leave them to marinate for 1 hour turning them over a few times. Reserve the *tare*.

For the garnish cut the cucumber in a *kirichigai* style (see page 169), then set aside. Cut the tomato into eight wedges.

Place the skewers on a rack and place the kebabs under a pre-heated grill [broiler] or over charcoal on a barbecue. Reduce to a low or moderate heat and cook for about 8 to 10 minutes, until cooked through and well browned – the edges of the meat may be very slightly burnt. Turn the kebabs during cooking and brush them with the *tare*.

Arrange the kebabs on small individual plates and garnish with the cucumber and tomato. The food should be eaten as soon as it is cooked.
**Serves 4**

**Opposite page** *Top: Gomoku Mame (page 119); bottom: Renkon No Jigatsuo Ni (page 118)* **Overleaf** *Clockwise from top left: Toriniku Namba Maki (page 123), Chahan (page 132), Yaki Tori and Amdai Kogane Yaki (page 120)*

# Gyuniku No Tataki

—— *Grilled [Broiled] Beef* ——

(Illustrated opposite)

| METRIC/IMPERIAL | AMERICAN |
|---|---|
| 450 g/1 lb fillet of beef | 1 lb boneless sirloin steak |
| salt | salt |
| 1 teaspoon *sake* | 1 teaspoon *sake* |
| 1 teaspoon Japanese soy sauce | 1 teaspoon Japanese soy sauce |
| *Garnish* | *Garnish* |
| 8.75-cm/3¼-in piece Japanese yam | 3¼-in piece Japanese yam |
| 10-cm/4-in piece large white radish | 4-in piece large white radish |
| 4 spring onions | 4 scallions |
| 100 ml/4 fl oz *Ponzu Joyu* (page 156) to serve | ½ cup *Ponzu Joyu* (page 156) for serving |

Trim any fat from the beef and thread three long skewers through the meat as shown in the diagram. Hold the end of the skewers in one hand and sprinkle 1 tablespoon salt all over the meat. Hold the meat about 13 cm/5 in away from a very hot grill [broiler] and cook it quickly, turning the meat all the time until the surface changes colour. Alternatively, hold the meat over a gas flame or charcoal in a barbecue. Immediately immerse the meat in ice-cold water. Don't cook the meat too much. Dry the meat on absorbent kitchen paper and put it on a plate. Sprinkle the *sake* and soy sauce on the meat, then wrap it in cling film [plastic wrap] and chill.

For the garnish, peel and cut the yam in half crossways, then slice it lengthways into 5-mm/¼-in strips. Cut these lengthways into 5-mm/¼-in sticks and soak them in water. Peel the radish and follow the instructions on page 163 to cut it in a *sengiri* style. Remove the spring onion [scallion] roots and any bruised leaves, then wash and chop the rest finely and set it aside in a small bowl.

Cut the meat against the grain into 3-mm/⅛-in thick slices. Arrange the meat on a serving plate, then arrange the vegetables on the plate in an attractive layout.

Pour the *Ponzu Joyu* into four small individual bowls and add the chopped spring onions [scallions]. Serve this with the beef. **Serves 4**

**Note:** instead of the *Ponzu Joyu* you can serve Japanese soy sauce with *wasabi* or with fresh root ginger.

*Top: Hiyamugi (page 136); bottom: Gyuniko No Tataki*

# Men Rui

## —— *Snacks and Noodle Dishes* ——

Noodles are very popular in Japan because their flavour can be changed in many ways and they can be mixed with many different ingredients. These dishes are suitable for serving as simple meals, lunches or snacks.

Try to remember the following points when you have boiled Japanese noodles: rinse them once under running water and drain them in a sieve or colander. Once the noodles are cooked you must use them as soon as possible, otherwise they will swell up.

Make any dipping sauce which you are serving with noodles a little thicker than normal. You can also serve small portions of the following ingredients with noodle dishes: chopped spring onions [scallions], chilli powder, peeled and grated fresh root ginger, lightly roasted sesame seeds, peeled and grated white radish, powdered dried bonito fish and slivers of
*wasabi* (Japanese green mustard).

# Oyako Donburi

###### —— *Rice with Chicken and Egg* ——

| METRIC/IMPERIAL | AMERICAN |
|---|---|
| 425 g/15 oz long-grain rice | 2¼ cups long-grain rice |
| 2 chicken leg joints or 225 g/8 oz | 2 chicken legs-with-thighs or ½ lb |
| silverside or topside | flank steak |
| 3 dried *shiitake* | 3 dried *shiitake* |
| 1 onion | 1 onion |
| 4 eggs, beaten | 4 eggs, beaten |
| *Kake Jiru* | *Kake Jiru* |
| 7 g/¼ oz dried bonito fish | ¼ oz dried bonito fish |
| 4 tablespoons Japanese soy sauce | ¼ cup Japanese soy sauce |
| 4 tablespoons *mirin* | ¼ cup *mirin* |
| 7½ teaspoons sugar | 7½ teaspoons sugar |
| 3 spring onions to garnish | 3 scallions for garnish |

Steam the rice following the instructions on page 23; this is to be served hot with the other prepared ingredients.

Prepare the chicken following the instructions on page 159, then remove and discard the skin. Cut the chicken meat across into 1-cm/½-in pieces. If you are using the beef, trim any fat from the meat and slice it thinly against the grain into pieces measuring 3-cm/1¼-in square. You may find it easier to slice the beef if it is half frozen.

Soak the dried *shiitake* in warm water for 20 minutes, remove and discard the stems and lightly squeeze the caps, then thinly slice them. Peel the onion and cut it in half vertically, then slice it thinly. Put all the *kake jiru* ingredients in a saucepan. Pour in 260 ml/8½ fl oz water [1 cup] and bring to the boil over a low to moderate heat. Turn off the heat, then strain the sauce through a fine sieve.

For the garnish remove the spring onion [scallion] roots and any bruised leaves, then wash the rest and cut it at a slant into 3-mm/⅛-in lengths. Set aside for later use.

Put all the prepared ingredients in a saucepan and pour in the *kake jiru*. Bring to the boil, then put a lid on the pan and simmer gently for 2 to 3 minutes. Remove the lid and pour the beaten eggs into the pan. Put the lid back on top and simmer gently for a further 1 to 2 minutes – do not overcook the eggs.

To serve, put the hot steamed rice in four small individual bowls, then spoon the other ingredients on top. Finally sprinkle the spring onions [scallions] on top of the ingredients. Serve immediately – the food should be eaten as soon as it is cooked. **Serves 4**

# Chahan

—— *Fried Rice with Vegetables* ——

(Illustrated on pages 126/127)

| METRIC/IMPERIAL | AMERICAN |
|---|---|
| 425 g/15 oz long-grain rice | $2\frac{1}{4}$ cups long-grain rice |
| 100 g/4 oz cooked ham | $\frac{1}{4}$ lb cooked ham |
| 3 spring onions | 3 scallions |
| 4 eggs | 4 eggs |
| 3 tablespoons lard | 3 tablespoons lard |
| salt and pepper | salt and pepper |
| 1 tablespoon *sake* | 1 tablespoon *sake* |
| 2 tablespoons Japanese soy sauce | 2 tablespoons Japanese soy sauce |

Steam the rice following the instructions on page 23. Fluff up the grains, then leave the rice in the open saucepan to cool. You must use cold rice for *Chahan* otherwise it will become damp.

Cut the ham into pieces about 1 cm/$\frac{1}{2}$ in square. Remove the spring onion [scallion] roots and any bruised leaves, then wash and finely chop the rest. Beat the eggs thoroughly.

Heat the lard in a big saucepan. Allow it to become smoking hot then add the beaten eggs and leave them until half set, then scramble them immediately but being careful not to break up the scrambled eggs too much. Add the ham, the chopped spring onions [scallions], $\frac{1}{2}$ teaspoon salt and pepper to taste. Reduce the heat to moderate and stir-fry for 1 minute, then add the rice to the pan and stir-fry continuously for another 1 minute. Pour in the *sake* and stir for a few moments. Finally pour the soy sauce into the pan and stir-fry for a further 30 seconds. When you add the *sake* and the soy sauce to the pan, pour them in around the sides of the pan or any spaces on the bottom: this method encourages these ingredients to give off their aroma.

To serve, put the rice on individual plates, arranging the food so that all the ingredients show distinctly. The food should be eaten as soon as it is cooked. **Serves 4**

**Note:** fried rice should be light and dry. You can also add peeled cooked prawns or shrimps, chopped green or sweet red peppers or a variety of other ingredients to this dish.

# Yakisoba

*—— Fried Noodles ——*

| METRIC/IMPERIAL | AMERICAN |
|---|---|
| 350 g/12 oz dried medium egg noodles (chow mein noodles) | $\frac{3}{4}$ lb dried medium-size egg noodles (chow mein noodles) |
| 6 tablespoons oil | 6 tablespoons oil |
| salt and pepper | salt and pepper |
| 200 g/7 oz cabbage | $\frac{1}{2}$ lb cabbage |
| 100 g/4 oz cooked ham | $\frac{1}{4}$ lb cooked ham |
| 1 onion | 1 onion |
| $\frac{1}{2}$ green pepper | $\frac{1}{2}$ green pepper |
| *Sauce* | *Sauce* |
| 50 ml/2 fl oz brown sauce | $\frac{1}{4}$ cup steak sauce |
| $7\frac{1}{2}$ teaspoons tomato ketchup | $7\frac{1}{2}$ teaspoons tomato ketchup |
| 4 eggs to garnish | 4 eggs for garnish |

Break the noodles into a saucepan of boiling water. Bring back to the boil and boil for about 6 to 7 minutes. Drain thoroughly. Heat a saucepan, pour in 3 tablespoons of the oil, allow it to become hot and stir-fry the noodles. Add 1 teaspoon salt and pepper to taste, then continue to stir-fry for 1 minute. Transfer the noodles to a big plate.

Remove the thicker stem parts and any bruised leaves from the cabbage, then cut the good part of the cabbage into shreds measuring 2 × 1 cm/$\frac{3}{4}$ × $\frac{1}{2}$ in. Cut the ham into pieces about the same size as the cabbage. Peel and cut the onion in half, then slice it thinly lengthways. Remove the stalk, pith and seeds from the green pepper, then cut it across into three and cut these pieces lengthways into 1-cm/$\frac{1}{2}$-in wide strips.

Mix all the ingredients for the sauce in a small bowl. Heat another 1–2 tablespoons of the oil in a frying pan. Lightly fry the eggs, then keep them warm.

Heat the saucepan, pour in the remaining 1 tablespoon oil and allow it to become hot. Stir-fry the cabbage, onion, pepper and ham. Add $\frac{1}{2}$ teaspoon salt and pepper to taste, then stir-fry for 1 to $1\frac{1}{2}$ minutes, or until the onion becomes translucent. Put the noodles in the pan and continue to stir-fry for 1 minute. Add the sauce mixture and stir-fry for a final $\frac{1}{2}$ to 1 minute.

Transfer the noodle mixture to individual plates and garnish each portion with a fried egg on top. The food should be eaten as soon as it is cooked.
**Serves 4**

# Tanabata Soumen

—— *Fine White Noodles with Vegetables* ——

| METRIC/IMPERIAL | AMERICAN |
| --- | --- |
| 350 g/12 oz whole uncooked prawns or shrimps | $\frac{3}{4}$ lb raw shrimp |
| 5 tablespoons plus 2 teaspoons *sake* | 5 tablespoons plus 2 teaspoons *sake* |
| salt | salt |
| 3 dried *shiitake* | 3 dried *shiitake* |
| 2 teaspoons Japanese soy sauce | 2 teaspoons Japanese soy sauce |
| 2 teaspoons sugar | 2 teaspoons sugar |
| 3 chicken leg joints | 3 chicken legs-with-thighs |
| 2 eggs | 2 eggs |
| 100 g/4 oz mange-tout peas | $\frac{1}{4}$ lb snow or sugar peas |
| 300 g/11 oz dry *soumen* (Japanese fine white noodles) | $\frac{3}{4}$ lb *somen* (fine white vermicelli) |
| *Dipping Sauce* | *Dipping Sauce* |
| 100 ml/4 fl oz *mirin* | $\frac{1}{2}$ cup *mirin* |
| 100 ml/4 fl oz Japanese soy sauce | $\frac{1}{2}$ cup Japanese soy sauce |
| 7 g/$\frac{1}{4}$ oz dried bonito fish | $\frac{1}{4}$ oz dried bonito fish |
| 3 spring onions | 3 scallions |
| 25 g/1 oz fresh root ginger | 1 oz fresh ginger root |

First make the dipping sauce: put the *mirin* in a saucepan and bring it to the boil over a moderate heat. Immediately add the soy sauce, bonito fish and 400 ml/14 fl oz [1$\frac{3}{4}$ cups] water. Bring to the boil, strain the sauce through a sieve and leave to cool. Remove the spring onion [scallion] roots and any bruised leaves, then wash and finely chop the remainder. Peel and grate the ginger. Set these ingredients aside.

Put the prawns [shrimp] in a saucepan. Pour in enough water to just cover them, then add 2 tablespoons of the *sake* and $\frac{1}{2}$ teaspoon salt to the pan. Bring to the boil, then simmer gently until the prawns [shrimp] become clear pink. Turn off the heat and leave the prawns [shrimp] in the pan to cool.

Soak the dried *shiitake* in warm water for 20 minutes. Remove and discard their stems and lightly squeeze the caps, then slice these thinly. Put the *shiitake* in a saucepan and add 100 ml/4 fl oz [$\frac{1}{2}$ cup] water. Pour in the soy sauce, 2 teaspoons of the *sake* and the sugar, then bring to the boil and simmer gently stirring continuously until most of the liquid has evaporated. Leave to cool.

Prepare the chicken following the instructions on page 59. Put the chicken meat in a dish suitable for steaming, then sprinkle with $\frac{1}{2}$ teaspoon salt and the remaining *sake*. Heat a steamer. When plenty of steam builds up put the dish in the steamer and put a tight-fitting lid on top. Reduce to a moderate heat and steam for 15 to 20 minutes. Remove the chicken and allow it to cool in its juices. Remove the chicken skin and discard this, then cut the meat into medium-sized pieces.

Prepare the eggs following the instructions for *Kinshi Tamago* (see page 156). Remove the stalks and any strings from the mange-touts [snow peas], then put them into boiling salted water. Bring to the boil, then boil for 2 minutes. Drain and soak in fresh water to cool. Drain the peas in a sieve then cut them thinly into slanting slices.

Add the *soumen* to a saucepan of boiling water. Bring back to the boil and cook for 4 to 5 minutes. Drain and soak in cold water for 30 seconds to cool. Do not soak the noodles too long otherwise they will swell up.

Put the drained noodles on to individual plates, then arrange the drained prawns [shrimp], chicken, *shiitake* and mange-tout [snow peas] on top, keeping them separate. Make the arrangement of ingredients look as attractive and neat as possible; remember that presentation is very important. Finally put the eggs in the centre. Pour the prepared dipping sauce into small individual bowls, adding the chopped spring onions [scallions] and the ginger. Serve the noodle dish cold, with the dipping sauce.
**Serves 4**

# Hiyamugi

—— *Cold White Noodles* ——

(Illustrated on page 129)

| METRIC/IMPERIAL | AMERICAN |
|---|---|
| 400 g/14 oz dried *hiyamugi* (Japanese medium-size white noodles) | 1 lb *hiyamugi* (medium-size white noodles) |
| *Dipping Sauce* | *Dipping Sauce* |
| 100 ml/4 fl oz *mirin* | $\frac{1}{2}$ cup *mirin* |
| 100 ml/4 fl oz Japanese soy sauce | $\frac{1}{2}$ cup Japanese soy sauce |
| 7 g/$\frac{1}{4}$ oz dried bonito fish | $\frac{1}{4}$ oz dried bonito fish |
| 3 spring onions | 3 scallions |
| 25 g/1 oz fresh root ginger | 1 oz fresh ginger root |
| *Garnish* | *Garnish* |
| 1 tomato | 1 tomato |
| 5-cm/2-in piece cucumber | 2-in piece cucubmer |
| 1 egg | 1 egg |

First make the dipping sauce: pour the *mirin* into a saucepan and bring it to the boil over a moderate heat. Then add the soy sauce and bonito fish to the pan. Pour in 400 ml/14 fl oz [1$\frac{3}{4}$ cups] water, bring to the boil and strain immediately through a fine sieve. Leave to cool. Remove the spring onion [scallion] roots and any bruised leaves, then wash and finely chop the rest. Peel and grate the ginger. Set these ingredients aside.

Prepare the ingredients for the garnish: cut the tomato into eight wedges. Peel the cucumber then cut it across into 2-mm/$\frac{1}{10}$-in thick slices. Cook the egg following the instructions for *Usuyaki Tamago* (see page 155), then cut it into 0.5 × 3-cm/$\frac{1}{4}$ × 1$\frac{1}{4}$-in pieces. Add the *hiyamugi* to a saucepan of boiling water. Bring back to the boil then cook for 7 to 8 minutes. Soak the noodles in cold water for 30 seconds to cool. Do not soak too long otherwise the noodles will swell up.

To serve, put the noodles in large individual glass bowls, then fill with cold water, arrange the garnishing ingredients in an attractive pattern on top. You may float some ice-cubes on the water. Pour the dipping sauce into small individual bowls, adding the chopped spring onions [scallions] and the ginger. Serve this sauce with the noodles. The food should be served as soon as it is prepared, otherwise the noodles will swell up. The noodles are lifted out of the water and eaten with a little of the sauce. **Serves 4**

# Tsuke Mono

## *—— Pickles ——*

Many different kinds of pickles are served in Japan. They are made from vegetables, seafood, meat, eggs or *tofu*. The ingredients are marinated in special sauces or simply with salt. Food has been preserved by pickling for centuries but nowadays many varieties of very good commercially produced pickles are widely available in Western countries as well as within Japan itself. This chapter offers recipes for simple pickles which you can make at home.

## Daikon, Daikon Ba Shio Zuke

### *—— Salted Large White Radish ——*

| METRIC/IMPERIAL | AMERICAN |
|---|---|
| 1 large white radish | 1 large white radish |
| 150 g/5 oz large white radish leaves | 5 oz large white radish leaves |
| 20 g/$\frac{3}{4}$ oz salt | 1$\frac{1}{2}$ tablespoons salt |

Cut the radish following the instructions for the *sen roppon* technique (see page 163). Wash the leaves thoroughly in few changes of clean water and remove any bruised parts. Chop the leaves finely.

Put the vegetables in a bowl, and sprinkle with 7 g/$\frac{1}{4}$ oz [$\frac{1}{2}$ tablespoon] of the salt, then stir for a few minutes. Squeeze the vegetables and pour off the water. Put the vegetables back in the bowl and sprinkle in the remaining salt. Put a small plate on top of the vegetables and put a 1 kg/2$\frac{1}{4}$ lb weight on the plate. Leave for at least 1 day.

This pickle can still be eaten after about 4 or 5 days, but if you leave the pickles too long they will become very salty.

# Shoga Amazu Zuke

—— *Ginger Pickle* ——

| METRIC/IMPERIAL | AMERICAN |
|---|---|
| 225 g/8 oz fresh root ginger (select young ginger) | $\frac{1}{2}$ lb fresh ginger root (select young ginger) |
| *Vinegar Dressing* | *Vinegar Dressing* |
| 150 ml/$\frac{1}{4}$ pint rice vinegar | $\frac{2}{3}$ cup rice vinegar |
| 2 tablespoons sugar | 2 tablespoons sugar |

Pour the vinegar into a small saucepan. Add 100 ml/4 fl oz [$\frac{1}{2}$ cup] water and the sugar. Boil over a low heat until the sugar has dissolved, then stand the pan in a bowl of cold water to cool.

Peel and slice the ginger thinly with the grain. Put the ginger slices in the vinegar dressing and leave to marinate for 1 week. You can keep this type of pickle for 2 to 3 months.

# Kyuri No Ichiya Zuke

—— *Cucumber Pickles* ——

| METRIC/IMPERIAL | AMERICAN |
|---|---|
| 2 cucumbers | 2 cucumbers |
| 20 g/$\frac{3}{4}$ oz salt | 1$\frac{1}{2}$ tablespoons salt |

Wash the cucumbers, quarter them lengthways, then cut the pieces in half crossways. Put the pieces in a bowl and sprinkle the salt on top. Put a small plate on the cucumber and put a 1-kg/2$\frac{1}{4}$-lb weight on the plate. Leave to marinate overnight. Squeeze the cucumber lightly and cut it into 3.5-cm/1$\frac{1}{2}$-in lengths. This pickle can be stored in an airtight container for up to 1 week.

# Wagashi

## —— *Sweets* ——

Japanese do not normally eat dessert after a meal. Sweets are eaten with tea as a between-meals snack. Although sweets are readily available in cake shops or supermarkets, they are rarely made at home.

Children and young people often prefer European-style cakes but traditional Japanese sweets are still popular with the older generation. Special sweets are available during festival periods, and people still make this type of speciality food.

This chapter introduces some Japanese sweets which are popular and easy to make.

## Zenzai

#### —— *Aduki Bean Soup with Sticky Rice Cake* ——

| METRIC/IMPERIAL | AMERICAN |
|---|---|
| 110 g/$4\frac{1}{4}$ oz dried *azuki* | $\frac{2}{3}$ cup dried *azuki* |
| 75 g/3 oz sugar | 6 tablespoons sugar |
| pinch of salt | pinch of salt |
| 8 (2.5 × 3-cm/1 × $1\frac{1}{4}$-in) pieces *mochi* | 8 (1 × $1\frac{1}{4}$-in) pieces *mochi* |

Discard any damaged *azuki*, then soak the rest in plenty of water for at least 12 hours. Drain the *azuki* and put them in a saucepan and pour in enough water to two-thirds fill the pan. Bring to the boil, then pour off the water. Two-thirds fill with fresh water and bring to the boil, then simmer until the *azuki* are tender – about 1 hour. Top up with water as required.

Drain the *azuki* in a sieve, reserving the cooking liquid into a bowl. Then return the beans to the pan. Make up the cooking liquid to 400 ml/14 fl oz [$1\frac{3}{4}$ cups] with boiling water, then pour it into the pan. Add the sugar and salt, and bring to the boil. Simmer gently while you prepare the *mochi*.

Put the *mochi* under a preheated grill [broiler] and cook under a low to moderate heat until the *mochi* become crisp and expanded. Turn the *mochi* over and grill [broil] the other side; take care not to burn it. Pour the *azuki* soup into small individual bowls and put the two pieces of *mochi* in each portion. Serve hot.

# Dorayaki

—— *Sweet Aduki Pancakes [Crêpes]* ——

| METRIC/IMPERIAL | AMERICAN |
|---|---|
| 75 g/3 oz dried *azuki* | ½ cup dried *azuki* |
| 100 g/4 oz sugar | ½ cup sugar |
| pinch of salt | pinch of salt |
| 20 g/¾ oz margarine | 1½ tablespoons margarine |
| 100 g/4 oz plain flour | 1 cup flour |
| 1 teaspoon bicarbonate of soda | 1 teaspoon baking soda |
| 1 egg | 1 egg |
| 100 ml/4 fl oz milk | ⅔ cup milk |

Discard any damaged *azuki*, then soak the others in plenty of water for at least 12 hours. Drain the beans and put them in a large saucepan. Fill the pan two-thirds full with water, then bring to the boil and pour off the water. Pour fresh water into the pan and bring to the boil, then boil gently until the *azuki* are soft, topping up with fresh water as required. This should take about 1 hour. Finally, allow the water to boil off until the beans are almost dry.

Add a quarter of the sugar and put the pan over a low to moderate heat. Beat thoroughly with a wooden spoon for 1 to 2 minutes. Repeat twice more without allowing the mixture to burn. Add the salt and continue to boil until any excess moisture has evaporated.

Melt the margarine: to do this, place the fat in a cup and heat the cup in a small bowl of boiling water. Mix the flour and the soda and sift these ingredients together twice. Separate the egg and whisk the egg white until stiff. Whisk the egg yolk with the milk and the remaining sugar in a mixing bowl. Gradually mix in the flour and the melted margarine making sure the ingredients are thoroughly combined and smooth. Finally add the whisked egg white and mix vigorously.

Heat 1 teaspoon oil in a small frying pan and use a pad of absorbent kitchen paper to wipe it over the bottom of the pan. Reduce the heat to low, pour in enough mixture to coat the bottom of the pan or to make a 7.5-cm/3-in diameter pancake [crêpe]. When bubbles appear in the mixture, use a large fish slice [spatula] to turn the pancake [crêpe] and fry the other side for 2 to 3 minutes. Fry the remaining mixture in the same way. Sandwich the cooked pancakes [crêpes] in pairs with the bean mixture. Put the pancakes [crêpes] on small individual plates and serve as soon as they are cooked. Alternatively, allow the pancakes [crêpes] to cool completely and serve cold.
**Serves 6**

# Mizu Yokan

*—— Set Aduki Bean Sweet ——*

(Illustrated on page 145)

| METRIC/IMPERIAL | AMERICAN |
|---|---|
| 110 g/4¼ oz dried *azuki* | ⅔ cup dried *azuki* |
| 75 g/3 oz sugar | 6 tablespoons sugar |
| pinch of salt | pinch of salt |
| 7 g/¼ oz agar agar | ¼ oz *kanten* or 1 envelope unflavored gelatin |

Discard any damaged *azuki*, then soak the others in plenty of water for at least 12 hours. Drain the beans and put them in a large saucepan. Fill the pan two-thirds full with water, then bring to the boil and pour off the water. Pour fresh water into the pan and bring to the boil, then boil gently until the *azuki* are soft, topping up with fresh water as required. This should take about 1 hour. Finally, allow the water to boil off until the beans are almost dry. Add one-third of the sugar and put the pan over a low to moderate heat. Beat thoroughly with a wooden spoon for 1 to 2 minutes. Repeat twice more without allowing the mixture to burn. Add the salt and continue to boil until any excess moisture has evaporated.

Wash the agar agar [*kanten*] under running water, then use your fingers to tear it up. Soak the pieces in water for 30 minutes. Wring out the pieces with both hands and put them into a saucepan. Add 250 ml/8 fl oz [1 cup] water to the pan, then bring to the boil over a moderate heat. When the agar agar [*kanten*] has dissolved completely, strain the liquid through a fine sieve. [If using gelatin, dissolve it in the liquid.]

Pour the agar agar [*kanten*] liquid back into a saucepan and bring to the boil over a low to moderate heat. Add the *azuki* to the pan, then stir for 1 minute to thoroughly mix in the *azuki*. Remove the pan from the heat and stand it in a bowl of cold water until the mixture is just tepid. Stir continuously and do not allow the mixture to cool down too much. Pour the *azuki* into a *nagashi kan* (see glossary) or into four or six small individual glasses. Chill in the refrigerator for 1 hour.

If the *azuki* was set in a *nagashi kan*, then remove it and cut it into 5 × 2.5-cm/2 × 1-in rectangles. Put these pieces on small individual plates. If you use glasses, serve the sweet straight from them. **Serves 4 to 6**

# Fruits Mitsumame

—— *Fruit Dessert* ——

(Illustrated on page 145)

| METRIC/IMPERIAL | AMERICAN |
|---|---|
| 7 g/$\frac{1}{4}$ oz agar agar | $\frac{1}{4}$ oz *kanten* or 1 envelope unflavored |
| 100 g/4 oz plus 4$\frac{1}{2}$ teaspoons sugar | gelatin |
| 1 banana | $\frac{1}{2}$ cup plus 4$\frac{1}{2}$ teaspoons sugar |
| 2 slices canned pineapple | 1 banana |
| $\frac{1}{2}$ dessert apple | 2 slices canned pineapple |
| 4 sweet cherries or morello cherries | $\frac{1}{2}$ apple |
| (fresh or canned) | 4 cherries (fresh or canned) |

Wash the agar agar [*kanten*] under running water, then use your hands to shred the block. Soak the pieces in water for 30 minutes. Wring the agar agar [*kanten*] and put it in a saucepan. Add 300 ml/$\frac{1}{2}$ pint [1$\frac{1}{4}$ cups] water and the 4$\frac{1}{2}$ teaspoons sugar to the pan and bring to the boil over a moderate heat. When the agar agar [*kanten*] has dissolved completely, strain the liquid through a fine sieve. [If using gelatin dissolve it in the liquid with the sugar.] Pour the liquid into a *nagashi kan* (see glossary) and chill in the refrigerator for 1 hour. Remove the mixture from the container and cut it into 1-cm/$\frac{1}{2}$-in cubes.

Cut the banana into 1-cm/$\frac{1}{2}$-in slices and cut each slice of pineapple into eight pieces. Cut the half apple into four wedges then remove the cores. Score a V-shape in the middle of the skin in each wedge and peel back three-quarters of the skin lengthways to make apple rabbits (see page 169). Put the remaining sugar in a small saucepan and add 4 tablespoons water. Boil over a low to moderate heat until the sugar has dissolved, then stand the pan in a bowl of cold water to cool the syrup.

Reserve the apple and cherries, then mix all the other ingredients, tossing them together gently, and pour in the syrup. Transfer to small glass bowls and arrange the apple and the cherries on top. Serve cool. **Serves 4**

# Osechi Ryori

## —— *New Year's Day Cooking* ——

New Year's Day is the most important festival in Japan and traditionally people visit their family, friends and work colleagues. The festival (*Nenshi*) lasts from the first to the third day of January and it is both a thanksgiving for the previous year as well as an opportunity to wish people good luck for the coming year. An integral and very important part of these celebrations is the special food which is prepared in each household. The generic name for this type of food is *osechi ryori* and *sake* is usually served as an accompaniment.

*Osechi ryori* is normally arranged overlapping in boxes called *jubako* and it is possible to buy these meals already prepared in big food shops in Japan. This type of *osechi ryori* is very popular, especially with young people. *Osechi ryori* consists of several different dishes which have different meanings: *kazunoko* (the prosperity of future generations), *kuro mame* (personal good health) and *gomame* (good harvest).

All the recipes in this chapter are typical *osechi ryori* dishes but their arrangement is not traditional. The dishes would make an interesting buffet party as they are all served cold and they can be prepared well in advance. Preparing and serving authentic *osechi ryori* requires extensive training, so the rather informal approach which is adopted here is probably the most suitable for Western cooks.

# Kikuka Kabu

—— *Turnip Chrysanthemum* ——

METRIC/IMPERIAL
1 turnip
2 dried whole chillies
300 ml/½ pint vinegar dressing for
*Shoga Amazu Zuke* (page 138)

AMERICAN
1 turnip
2 dried hot peppers
1¼ cups vinegar dressing for *Shoga
Amazu Zuke* (page 138)

Peel and cut the turnip into 2.5-cm/1-in lengths, then cut each into a hexagon measuring 3 cm/1¼ in. in diameter. Cut these in a *kikuka giri* style (see page 169) and soak the pieces in salted water for 10 minutes. Drain the turnips.

Remove the stalk and seeds from the chilli [hot pepper], then cut it thinly crossways. Put the chilli [hot pepper] in the vinegar dressing and add the turnip. Leave to marinate for 2 hours. Serve with a few pieces of the chilli [hot pepper] picked out on top of the turnip. **Serves 10**

# Kohaku Kamaboko

—— *Red and White Japanese Fish Cake* ——

(Illustrated on pages 146/147)

METRIC/IMPERIAL
1 red and 1 white Japanese fish cake

AMERICAN
1 red and 1 white Japanese fish cake

Remove the boards from the fish cakes, then slice them into 1-cm/½-in wide pieces. Cut the pieces of the fish cake as shown in diagram 1, then twist them as shown in diagram 2. **Serves 10**

**Note:** the Japanese fish cakes are bought ready steamed. They can be purchased frozen, then defrosted ready to eat.

1 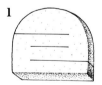    2

**Opposite Page** *Top: Mizu Yokan (page 141); bottom: Fruits Mitsumame (page 142)*
**Overleaf** *New year's Day Dishes, clockwise from top left: Toriniku No Yoro Ni (page 151), Kohaku Kamaboko, Salmon No Hosho Maki (page 150) and Ise Ebi No Sugata Yaki (page 149)*

# Ise Ebi No Sugata Yaki

*Grilled [Broiled] Lobster*

(Illustrated on pages 146/147)

| METRIC/IMPERIAL | AMERICAN |
|---|---|
| 2 lobsters | 2 lobsters |
| *Sauce 1* | *Sauce 1* |
| 1 teaspoon *mirin* | 1 teaspoon *mirin* |
| 2 teaspoons Japanese soy sauce | 2 teaspoons Japanese soy sauce |
| *Sauce 2* | *Sauce 2* |
| 1 tablespoons *sake* | 1 tablespoon *sake* |
| pinch of salt | pinch of salt |

Bring a large pan of water to a rapid boil. Add the lobsters and put a tight-fitting lid on the pan. Hold it down firmly. Boil for about 20 minutes or until the shell turns red. Drain the lobsters in a sieve or colander and leave to cool. Mix the ingredients for the sauces and keep them separate.

Trim the legs off with kitchen scissors. Crack and peel off the lobster shells, leaving the heads and tails in place. Thread two metal skewers through each lobster and brush both sauces over them. Grill [ broil] over a low heat, turning once and brushing with the sauces occasionally. The lobster will be ready after about 15 minutes. **Serves 10**

*Informal meal Menu 2*

# Salmon No Hosho Maki

*Rolled Salmon with Turnip Pickles*

(Illustrated on pages 146/147)

| METRIC/IMPERIAL | AMERICAN |
|---|---|
| 10 sliced turnip pickles | 10 sliced turnip pickles |
| 100 g/4 oz smoked salmon | $\frac{1}{4}$ lb smoked salmon |
| 1 tablespoon lemon juice | 1 tablespoon lemon juice |

Cut the turnip with a 10-cm/4-in round pastry cutter. Cut the *kombu* (which comes in the packet with the turnip pickles) into strips to make thongs.

Cut the salmon into ten pieces and sprinkle each with a little lemon juice. Roll up each piece of salmon and wrap the turnip around each roll, then tie neatly with the *kombu*. **Serves 10**

# Fukiyose Tamago

—— *Steamed Eggs* ——

| METRIC/IMPERIAL | AMERICAN |
|---|---|
| 10 eggs | 10 eggs |
| 6–8 tablespoons sugar | 6–8 tablespoons sugar |
| salt | salt |

Boil the eggs for about 12 minutes. Cut the eggs in half and remove their yolks. Press the whites and yolks separately through a sieve. Put half the sugar and $\frac{1}{2}$ teaspoon salt into the whites and add the remaining sugar with another $\frac{1}{2}$ teaspoon salt to the yolks. Spread the white evenly in a *nagashi kan* (see glossary), then spread the yolk evenly on top.

Heat a steamer. When there is plenty of steam, put the *nagashi kan* in the steamer and steam for 6 to 7 minutes over a moderate heat. Remove the eggs from the *nagashi kan*, leave to cool and cut into shapes with a small pastry cutter. **Serves 10**

# Toriniku No Yoro Ni

—— *Boiled Chicken* ——

(Illustrated on pages 146/147)

| METRIC/IMPERIAL | AMERICAN |
|---|---|
| 2 (15 × 20-cm/6 × 8-in) sheets *kombu* | 2 (6 × 8-in) sheets *kombu* |
| 7 g/¼ oz fresh root ginger | ¼ oz fresh ginger root |
| 2 chicken breasts | 1 whole chicken breast |
| cornflour for dusting | cornstarch for dredging |
| *Sauce* | *Sauce* |
| 4 tablespoons Japanese soy sauce | ¼ cup Japanese soy sauce |
| 3 tablespoons *mirin* | 3 tablespoons *mirin* |
| 2 tablespoons *sake* | 2 tablespoons *sake* |

Soak the *kombu* in water for 1 hour. Peel and grate the ginger, then squeeze it out to extract the ginger juice. Remove the bones and skin from the chicken. Cut open the chicken meat with a sharp knife to make thin wide slices. Sprinkle cornflour [cornstarch] over the meat and lay the slices flat on a *makisu* (bamboo blind). Put the *kombu* on the chicken and use the *makisu* as a guide to roll up the chicken. Unroll the *makisu* and skewer the chicken with cocktail sticks. Roll all the chicken slices in the same way.

Put the sauce ingredients in a saucepan. Bring to the boil, then put the chicken rolls in the pan. Reduce the heat to low or moderate and simmer gently until the meat is cooked – about 30 minutes. Finally add the ginger juice to the pan, then turn off the heat and leave to cool.

To serve, cut the cooled chicken rolls into 1.5-cm/¾-in slices. **Serves 10**

# Kuri Kinton

—— *Mashed Sweet Potato with Chestnuts* ——

| METRIC/IMPERIAL | AMERICAN |
|---|---|
| 575 g/1¼ lb sweet potatoes | 1 lb sweet potatoes |
| 250 g/9 oz sugar | 1 cup sugar |
| 2 tablespoons *mirin* | 2 tablespoons *mirin* |
| 12 chestnuts in heavy syrup | 12 canned chestnuts in heavy syrup |

Cut the sweet potatoes into 1-cm/½-in slices, peel and soak these in water for 3 to 4 hours. Cook them in boiling water until tender, then immediately press them through a sieve. This is easier if the slices are pressed through one by one.

Put the sugar in a saucepan, add 3 tablespoons water and bring to the boil. When all the sugar has dissolved reduce the heat, mix in the sweet potatoes and knead thoroughly. Add the *mirin* and continue to knead. Finally add the chestnuts to the pan and mix well. Transfer to individual bowls to serve. **Serves 10**

**Note:** chestnuts in syrup – marrons glacé – are available from many supermarkets and delicatessens.

# Cherry Kan

—— *Cherries with Jelly* ——

| METRIC/IMPERIAL | AMERICAN |
|---|---|
| 7 g/¼ oz agar agar | ¼ oz *kanten* or ½ envelope unflavored gelatin |
| 90 g/3¼ oz sugar | 6 tablespoons sugar |
| 1 teaspoon plum wine or red wine | 1 teaspoon plum wine or red wine |
| 1 (425-g/15-oz) can cherries, drained | 1 (16-oz) can cherries, drained |

Wash the agar agar [*kanten*] under running water, then use your fingers to tear it up. Soak the pieces in water for 30 minutes. Wring out the pieces with both hands and put them into a saucepan with 300 ml/½ pint [1¼ cups] water. Bring to the boil, add the sugar, then reduce the heat to low or moderate and add the wine. Immediately strain the liquid through a fine sieve. [If using gelatin, dissolve it in the liquid.]

Pour the agar agar [*kanten*] into individual foil cake cases. Put in the refrigerator and float the cherries on top when the mixture is half set. **Serves 4**

# Special Techniques

Japanese cooking has certain distinctive features. It is a mixture of uniquely Japanese ideas combined with foreign influences from China, Korea, Spain, Portugal and America. Japanese people enjoy eating fish, perhaps more than any other nation and their food is quite light in flavour. Compared with the cookery of other countries, Japanese cooking is not too oily.

In addition to these characteristics, Japanese cookery is artistic and full of variety in shape or form. Colour is important and food should be well matched.

Tableware is very important. There is an enormous variety of Japanese tableware: dishes and other items made of silver, pottery (china and porcelain) or glass. Japanese tableware is not like that found in China and Europe in that frequently, and preferably, all the dishes on a table will have different designs, but of course designs that harmonize well. The Western concept of a large dinner service would be regarded as being in rather bad taste, or at least showing a lack of imagination.

Japanese food has abundant decoration; for example, imitation flowers or a bunch of plum flowers are presented on a serving plate with a meal. This chapter offers some of the basic recipes and many of the essential techniques which you will have to follow in order to achieve authentic results.

## Ichiban Dashi

—— *Stock* ——

| METRIC/IMPERIAL | AMERICAN |
|---|---|
| 10-cm/4-in square dried *kombu* | 4-in square dried *kombu* |
| 7 g/$\frac{1}{4}$ oz dried bonito fish | $\frac{1}{4}$ oz dried bonito fish |

Wipe the *kombu* with a piece of absorbent kitchen paper. Put it into a saucepan and pour in 1 litre/1$\frac{3}{4}$ pints [1 quart] water. Bring to the boil very slowly over a low heat: this should take about 15 minutes. Add the bonito fish to the pan and turn off the heat. When the bonito fish starts to sink, strain the stock through a sieve or cloth.

# Sushi Meshi

—— *Sushi Rice* ——

| METRIC/IMPERIAL | AMERICAN |
|---|---|
| 425 g/15 oz Japanese rice | 2¼ cups Japanese rice |
| 725 ml/25 fl oz water | 3 cups water |
| *Awase Zu (Sushi Vinegar)* | *Awase Zu (Sushi Vinegar)* |
| 4 tablespoons rice vinegar | ¼ cup rice vinegar |
| 40 g/1½ oz sugar | 3 tablespoons sugar |
| 7 g/¼ oz salt | 1½ teaspoons salt |

Put all the *Awase Zu* ingredients in a saucepan, warm up over a low heat until the sugar dissolves. Remove from the heat and allow to cool.

Wash the rice in a bowl with cold running water: partly fill the bowl with water and stir the rice gently. Pour off the water and repeat two or three times. Drain the rice in a sieve or colander, leaving it for about 30 to 60 minutes. This allows the rice to absorb some water and partially soften the grains.

Put the rice in a heavy-based saucepan which has a tight-fitting lid and add the measured water. Cover the saucepan, then bring to the boil over the maximum heat and wait until steam begins to appear around the edge of the lid. Lower the heat and simmer the rice gently for 12 to 13 minutes, keeping the lid tightly on the pan all the time. Increase the heat to the maximum available and cook the rice for a further 10 seconds, then remove the saucepan from the heat. If you are cooking on an electric stove it is very important to use the maximum setting and to allow the ring to reach its maximum heat before timing the 10 seconds. Leave the saucepan, off the heat, with the lid still firmly on top for about 5 to 10 minutes.

Remove the lid and put the rice in a big bowl or big baking tray. Fluff up the rice lightly then pour in the *Awase Zu*. Pour the vinegar mixture over a wooden spoon evenly into the rice. Fluff up the rice while fanning it quickly with a piece of paper (this removes the alcohol from the vinegar as quickly as possible and produces shiny rice) until most of the steam disappears. Leave to become tepid.

**Note:** you should always use Japanese rice for *sushi* and always cover *sushi meshi* with a damp cloth until all the ingredients are ready. Do not allow the rice to dry out.

# Niban Dashi

—— *Light Stock* ——

| METRIC/IMPERIAL | AMERICAN |
|---|---|
| 1 tablespoon dried bonito fish strained ingredients from *Ichiban Dashi* (page 153) | 1 tablespoon dried bonito fish strained ingredients from *Ichiban Dashi* (page 153) |

Put the bonito fish and the strained ingredients in a saucepan. Pour in 1 litre/1¾ pints [1 quart] water and cook in the same way as the *Ichiban Dashi* stock.

# Usuyaki Tamago

—— *Thin Fried Egg* ——

| METRIC/IMPERIAL | AMERICAN |
|---|---|
| 4 eggs | 4 eggs |
| salt | salt |
| oil for cooking | oil for cooking |

Beat the eggs thoroughly with a pinch of salt. Allow a frying pan to become hot, then pour in 1 tablespoon oil. Wipe the oil around the pan with a piece of folded absorbent kitchen paper. The oil should be spread around the bottom of the pan thinly and evenly. Reduce to a moderate heat, pour some of the egg in the pan and immediately tilt the pan until the egg covers the bottom. Allow the egg to set, turn it over and fry for a few seconds on the other side.

Lift the egg on to a chopping board. Repeat for the remaining egg, turning out the sheets on top of each other. This should yield five to seven sheets.

# Kinshitamago (or Sengiritamago)
—— *Shredded Egg* ——

| METRIC/IMPERIAL | AMERICAN |
| --- | --- |
| 4 eggs | 4 eggs |
| salt | salt |

Follow the instructions for *Usuyaki Tamago* (page 155). Cut the cooked egg into 4-cm/1½-in wide long strips, then stack up some of the strips. Cut across the strips to make smaller thin strips. Repeat for the remaining strips.

# Ponzu Joyu
—— *Dipping Sauce* ——

| METRIC/IMPERIAL | AMERICAN |
| --- | --- |
| 3 tablespoons *mirin* | 3 tablespoons *mirin* |
| 200 ml/7 fl oz fresh lemon juice | 1 cup fresh lemon juice |
| 150 ml/¼ pint rice vinegar | ⅔ cup rice vinegar |
| 250 ml/8 fl oz Japanese soy sauce | 1 cup Japanese soy sauce |
| 7 g/¼ oz dried bonito fish | ¼ oz dried bonito fish |
| 5-cm/2-in square *kombu* | 2-in square *kombu* |

Put the *mirin* in a small saucepan and bring to the boil over a moderate heat, then immediately turn off the heat. Mix the *mirin* with all the other ingredients in a bowl. Cover and leave for 1 day. Strain the ingredients into a jar and leave for about 1 month in a dark cool place.

# Gomai Oroshi

*—— To obtain four fillets and edible bones from flat fish. ——*

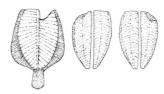

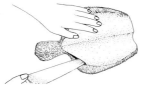

1 Remove the fish head and wash. Lay your hand flat on the fish and cut around both sides with a sharp knife.

2 Slice the fish lightly straight down over the backbone working from head to tail.

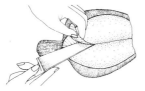

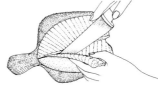

3 Cutting at an angle and as near to the bone as possible, remove the left quarter.

4 Turn the fish around and remove the second quarter (fillet) in the same way.

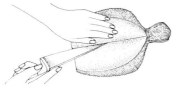

5 Turn the fish over and cut lightly down the backbone from tail to head (as before).

6 Remove the left-hand fillet in the same way as you cut off the first fillet.

7 Turn the fish over and remove the last fillet. The bones which remain can be used if required for edible bones in any recipe.

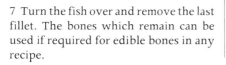

# Sanmai Oroshi

—— *To cut two fish fillets from round fish, for example mackerel.* ——

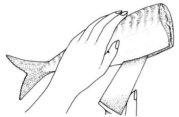

1 Cut the fish through to the bone from the head to the tail.

2 Turn the fish over and cut down the back through to the bone from the tail to the head.

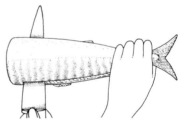

3 Cut through the fish between the flesh and bones from the tail to the head leaving the tail joint intact.

4 Hold the tail with one hand and remove the flesh, cutting carefully to keep all the bones together. Lift off the fillet, cutting it at the tail end.

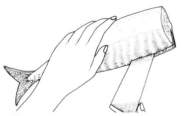

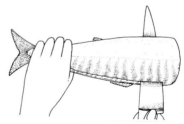

5 After removing the first fillet, turn the fish over and cut the fish from the head to the tail, down the back.

6 Turn the fish around and remove the second fillet as before, cutting the fish away from the bones.

# Breadcrumbs

Cut fresh white bread into 2.5-cm/1-in cubes and make these into breadcrumbs in a blender or food processor. Spread the breadcrumbs thinly and evenly on a baking tray and put them in a moderately hot oven (200 C, 400 F, gas 6) until they are dry. Do not allow the crumbs to become too dark. The breadcrumbs should not be too fine – coarse breadcrumbs are satisfactory.

When breadcrumbs are listed in any of the recipes, this is how they should be made.

**Deep frying:** to check the temperature of the oil. Drop a breadcrumb into the oil. When the breadcrumb sinks to the bottom, then quickly comes back to the surface the temperature is about 160 C/320 F. If the breadcrumb sinks about halfway into the oil and comes back to the surface, the temperature is about 170 C/340 F. If the bread does not sink at all the oil is about 180 C/355 F.

# Tebiraki

*—— Preparation of small whole fish for example sardines or sprats. ——*

1 Wash the fish in salted water, removing any scales by rubbing the skin with your hand.

2 Cut off the head and cut down the belly from the head to the tail. Remove the guts then rinse the inside of the fish with running water. Drain thoroughly on absorbent kitchen paper.

3 To bone the fish, run the nail of the left thumb firmly down the length of the bone. Start at the head end, then slide the thumb down to the tail and open up the fish. Insert the thumb in under the bone then slide down to the tail as before. The bone should come away from the meat.

4 Snap the bone at the tail joint, pick up the bone then pull it out towards the head. Cut off the tail and discard the bones and tails.

# Chicken Preparation

Make a cut up the side of the chicken leg right through the meat to the bone, removing all the meat. Sever the sinews from the joint and remove the bone from the flesh. The chicken is now ready for use as required.

# Squid Preparation

*Method 1*

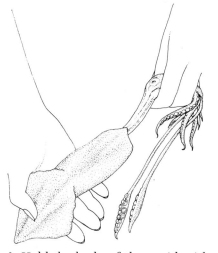

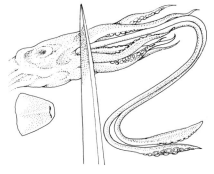

1 Hold the body of the squid with one hand and hold the tentacles in the other hand, then pull the legs away from the body (diagram 1). The head and legs will come away from the body.

3 Remove the long fine bone and all the internal organs, then wash the squid. Rub off the skin. Discard all the removed parts.

4 Cut off the flap sections (diagram 3). Cut the legs from the head and discard the head. Save the legs and the flap sections for making certain recipes.

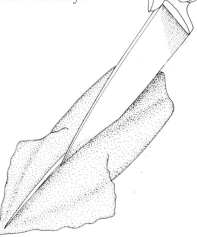

2 Cut the body of the squid lengthways and open it out flat (diagram 2).

*Method 2*

1 Hold the body of the squid with one hand and hold the legs in the other hand, then pull the legs from the body. The head and legs will come away from the body.

2 Wash the squid, remove the bone and all the internal organs from the body. Rub off the skin, then discard all the removed parts. Wash the squid thoroughly and use as required.

# Cutting Techniques for Sashimi

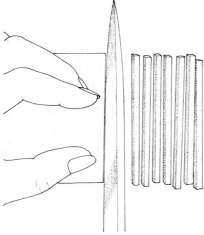

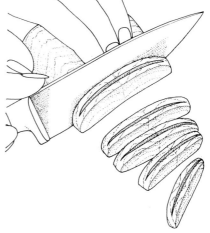

**Ito Zukuri**
When you use thick squid, slice off 2 or 3 pieces and cut them thinly crossways.

**Yae Zukuri (Kirikake Zukuri)**
Alternately cut part way and fully through the fish.

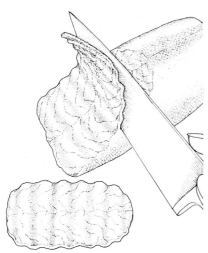

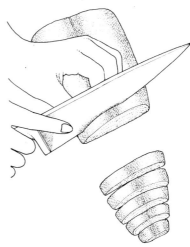

**Sazanami Zukuri**
Slice the fish, making 30° zig-zag cuts down each slice.

**Hira Zukuri**
With the skin side of the fish on top, make clean cuts, pulling the knife towards you. Push the cut fish to the right slightly with the blade when cutting.

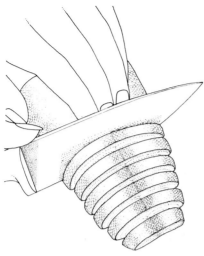

### Hiki Zukuri

This technique is the same as Hira Zukuri except that the fish is not pushed sideways as it is cut.

### Sogi Zukuri

Cut the fish, holding the knife at an angle of about 20° to the surface. Make the slices about 3–5 mm/$\frac{1}{8}$–$\frac{1}{4}$ in thick.

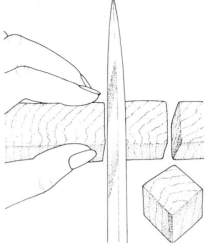

### Kaku Zukuri

Cut the fish into cubes.

*Arranging Sashimi*

**Hushi Mori:** Arrange an odd number of *Hira Zukuri* or *Hiki Zukuri* on a plate.

**Sugi Mori:** Make a small heap of Ito Zukuri on a plate.

**Maze Mori:** Arrange a selection of different types of *sashimi* on a plate. Pay particular attention to harmony of flavour and shape.

**Ran Mori:** Arrange the chosen Sashimi naturally and casually on the plate with the rear of the arrangement higher than the front.

# Kihon Giri – Cutting Techniques

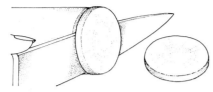

### Wa Giri (ring cut)
Slice evenly into ring shapes. For large white radish or carrot.

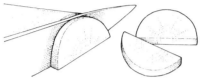

### Hangetsu Giri
Cut in half vertically then slice crossways.

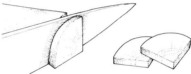

### Icas Giri (maiden hair tree leaf cut)
Quarter vertically, then slice crossways.

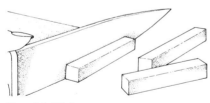

### Hyoshi Giri
Cut into rectangles measuring 4–5 × 1 cm/$1\frac{1}{2}$–2 × $\frac{1}{2}$ in.

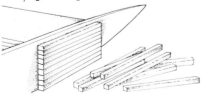

### Sen Roppon
Cut into matchstick size strips.

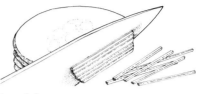

### Sengiri
(A) Peel and cut the ingredient at a slant and as thinly as you can. The slices will slide over each other naturally. Cut the slices again and in the same direction as before to make very fine strips slimmer than matchsticks.
(B) For Bamboo shoots or similar, peel and cut across into 3–3.5-cm/$1\frac{1}{4}$–$1\frac{1}{2}$-in slices then slice as thinly as you can lengthways. Cut these pieces into very fine strips as for (A).

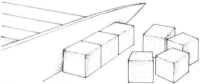

### Sainome Giri
Cut into 1-cm/$\frac{1}{2}$-in cubes.

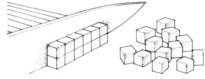

### Arare Giri
Cut into 5-mm/$\frac{1}{4}$-in cubes.

### Mijin Giri
Prepare the ingredients, as for *sengiri*, then cut across the strips to chop finely.

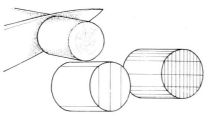

**Tanzaku Giri**
Cut across into 5-cm/2-in slices, then cut these lengthways into 1-cm/½-in pieces together and cut them lengthways again into thin pieces.

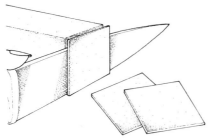

**Shikishi Giri**
Slice thinly crossways into 2.5-cm/1-in squares.

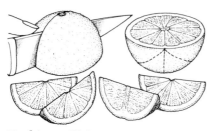

**Kushigata Giri**
Cut into eight wedges.

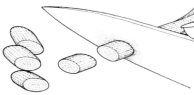

**Naname Giri**
Cut slices obliquely (at a slant); for cucumber, spring onions [scallions] or leeks.

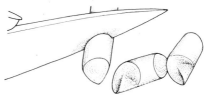

**Ran Giri**
Holding the knife at an angle, cut the ingredients, turning the piece around as you cut but keep the knife in the same position. Cut different ingredients to the same size before you start.

**Sasagaki**
Cut into long pieces then whittle pieces off the end into a bowl of water. A technique similar to sharpening a pencil using a knife.

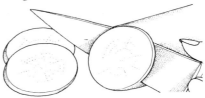

**Sogi Giri**
Hold the knife at a slant and cut the food into thin slices.

**Katsura Muki**
For cylindrical ingredients, hold the food in your left hand and cut it very thinly (as though you were peeling it) into one long, curled strip.

**Opposite page:** *Small Dinner Party Menu 1;* **Overleaf:** *Banquet Menu 1*

# Kazari Giri

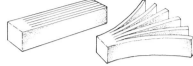

### Umeka Giri
For carrots. Cut into a pentagon, nick away the middle at each side then neatly peel away the material from the edge to round off the corners and make a flower shape.

### Suemiro Giri
Cut into rectangles, then make fine cuts into the piece. Leave these attached by about 5 mm/$\frac{1}{4}$ in at one end. Open the cuts out to make a fan shape.

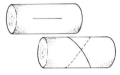

### Nejiri Ume
For carrots. Slice carrot prepared as for *umeka giri* into 5-mm/$\frac{1}{4}$-in slices. Cut from the middle out to make thin segments.

### Kirichigai
Making slanting cuts from the outside to the middle, on opposite sides of the ingredient.

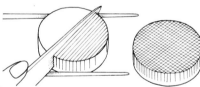

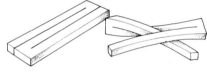

### Kikuka Giri
For turnips. Peel and cut into 2-cm/$\frac{3}{4}$-in wide slices. Hold chopsticks on both sides at the base of each slice, then make fine criss-cross cuts down as far as the chopsticks.

### Matsuba Giri
(A) Cut in a rectangular shape cut almost through into 3 strips and twist both ends.
(B) Cut in a rectangular shape then cut almost in half; open up.

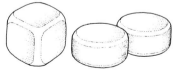

### Mentori
For large white radishes to keep the shape during boiling. Cut into cubes or cylinders then round off the corners.

### Apple Rabbit
Cut an apple into eight wedges. Score a deep V-shape in the skin and peel back the ends.

**Opposite page:** *Attractive presentation is important in Japanese cooking*

# Table Etiquette

### ——— To Use Chopsticks Correctly ———

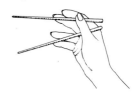

1 Rest the chopsticks across the palm of your hand, cushioning the thick ends between your thumb and index finger.

2 Support the end of one chopstick between your fourth and middle finger. Keep the chopstick nearest your thumb still.

3 Use your index finger to support and control the second chopstick, moving it towards the first one to close the gap between their points.

### ——— To Put Chopsticks Down ———

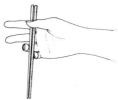

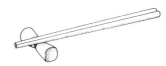

1 When you have finished eating, make sure your chopsticks are neatly placed together.

2 Place the narrow end of the chopsticks on the chopstick rest.

### ——— Chopsticks Etiquette ———

Do not use your chopsticks to search for ingredients.
Do not spear food with chopsticks.
Do not use chopsticks to shovel food into your mouth.
Do not pick one ingredient, then change your mind and put it down.
Do not be indecisive in picking up food.
Do not use chopsticks to pull a bowl or dish towards you.
Do not chew or lick your chopsticks.
Do not allow soup or juice to drip from your chopsticks.
Do not stick your chopsticks into the rice to stand them up instead of putting them down neatly. This signifies death in Japan.

## —— *How to eat Kaiseki Ryori with Sake* ——

There are three types of dinner menu: *honezen ryori*, *kaiseki ryori* and *kaiseki ryori with sake*. A normal dinner party at a restaurant would be either *kaiseki ryori* with *sake* or *honzen ryori*. Whether the meal is served course by course or all together the same etiquette applies in each case.

1 When *sake* is served with a starter you should have one mouthful of the *sake* before eating any of the food.
2 When you eat *sashimi* use a small plate to catch any drips of soy sauce.
3 You may use your fingers to shell seafood.
4 When eating salad, if the food is very juicy you should catch any drips with a small piece of paper.
5 You should serve yourself from the pickle bowl, then pass it to the next person.

## —— *To eat difficult foods* ——

1 *Chawan Mushi* (Steamed Egg) If the food is very hot hold the bowl with a saucer and use chopsticks or a spoon.
2 *Ebi No Yakimono* (Grilled Prawns [Broiled Shrimp]). Use your fingers to peel off the shells. Wipe your hands, then use chopsticks to eat the food.
3 *Yaki Hamaguri* (Grilled [Broiled] Clam). These are usually very hot so handle the clam with a piece of paper.
4 *Sakana No Sugata Yaki* (Grilled [Broiled] Whole Fish). Press the fish gently with your left hand to hold it in place, then remove and eat the fish with chopsticks. When the fish is finished put the bones in one corner of the dish.

## —— *Tea* ——

Japan has the famous tea ceremony, but for everyday tea drinking a far less formal style is normal. There are many ways of preparing tea but I will describe the popular *Sencha* method.

1 Pour boiling water into a pot (*Kyusu*) and a hot water jug.
2 Pour all the water from the pot into the cups.
3 Put tea leaves in the pot.
4 When most of the steam has disappeared from the hot water jug, pour the water into the pot. (Do not use boiling water for tea.)
5 Pour away the water in the cups.
6 Pour the tea into the warmed cups. You shouldn't leave any water in the pot. Pour fresh hot water into the pot and enjoy a second or third pot of tea.

# Menus

---

## Small Dinner Party Menus

| Menu 1 | Menu 2 |
|---|---|
| **Sliced Smoked Salmon with Lemon** | **Gohan**<br>*Steamed Rice* |
| **Suimono**<br>*Clear Soup* | **Suimono**<br>*Clear Soup* |
| **Shabu Shabu**<br>*Beef Nabe* | **Moriawase**<br>*Tempura* |
| **Kyuri To Wakame No Sunomono**<br>*Cucumber and Seaweed with Vinegar Dressing* | **Gyoza**<br>*Chinese-style Fried Meat Dumplings* |
| **Tsuke Mono**<br>*Pickles* | **Moyashi No Wasabi Ae**<br>*Bean Sprouts with Japanese Green Mustard* |
| | **Tsuke Mono**<br>*Pickles* |

# Banquet Menus

| Menu 1 | Menu 2 |
|--------|--------|

**Misoshiru**
*Soya Bean Paste Soup*

**Onigiri**
*Rice Balls*

**Yaki Niku**
*Korean-style Barbecue*

**Abura Age Maki**
*Fried Meat with Soya Bean
Cake Rolls*

**Tsuke Mono**
*Pickles*

**Osechi Ryori**
*New Year's Day Dishes*

**Suimono**
*Clear Soup*

**Seki Han**
*Rice with Red Beans*

**Tsuke Mono**
*Pickles*

# Menus for Informal Meals

| Menu 1 | Menu 2 |
|--------|--------|

**Takenoko Gohan**
*Rice with Bamboo Shoots*

**Misoshiru**
*Soya Bean Paste Soup*

**Shoga Yaki**
*Fried Pork with Ginger*

**Horenso No Ohitashi**
*Boiled Spinach*

**Tsuke Mono**
*Pickles*

**Gohan**
*Steamed Rice*

**Sukiyaki**
*Simmered Beef*

**Horenso No Ohitashi**
*Boiled Spinach*

**Tsuke Mono**
*Pickles*

# Index

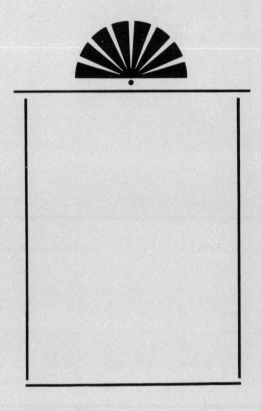